Hampshire Vol II
Edited by Steve Twelvetree

First published in Great Britain in 2005 by:
Young Writers
Remus House
Coltsfoot Drive
Peterborough
PE2 9JX
Telephone: 01733 890066
Website: www.youngwriters.co.uk

All Rights Reserved

© *Copyright Contributors 2004*

SB ISBN 1 84460 658 9

Foreword

Young Writers was established in 1991 and has been passionately devoted to the promotion of reading and writing in children and young adults ever since. The quest continues today. Young Writers remains as committed to engendering the fostering of burgeoning poetic and literary talent as ever.

This year's Young Writers competition has proven as vibrant and dynamic as ever and we are delighted to present a showcase of the best poetry from across the UK. Each poem has been carefully selected from a wealth of *Once Upon A Rhyme* entries before ultimately being published in this, our twelfth primary school poetry series.

Once again, we have been supremely impressed by the overall high quality of the entries we have received. The imagination, energy and creativity which has gone into each young writer's entry made choosing the best poems a challenging and often difficult but ultimately hugely rewarding task - the general high standard of the work submitted amply vindicating this opportunity to bring their poetry to a larger appreciative audience.

We sincerely hope you are pleased with our final selection and that you will enjoy *Once Upon A Rhyme Hampshire Vol II* for many years to come.

Contents

Fryern Junior School
- Megan Purkis (7) — 1
- Yasmin Bradshaw (7) — 1
- Shaun Moger (9) — 2
- Charley Cooper (9) — 2
- Lia Summers (9) — 3
- Kevin West (9) — 3
- Mitchell Steele (9) — 4
- Matthew Wenman (7) — 4
- Paige Edwards (9) — 5
- Lauren Tarrant (10) — 5
- Abbie Jackson (8) — 6
- Olivia Stone (8) — 6
- Katie Hodson (8) — 6
- Chad Mansergh (9) — 7
- Louise Giddings (8) — 7
- Emily Baker (8) — 7
- Ella Hannah (9) — 8
- Kate Pile (8) — 8
- Kira Whitton (8) — 8
- Daisy Trott (8) — 8
- Eleanor Bowles (9) — 9
- Sean Hopcroft (9) — 9
- Sara Osborne (8) — 9
- Amy Allsop (9) — 10
- Nadia Douglas (8) — 10
- Harry George (9) — 10
- Lauren Harding (9) — 11
- Lucy Ransom (9) — 11
- Kayleigh Gray (9) — 12
- Chloe Lebbern (9) — 12
- Benjamin Limbrick (9) — 13
- Faye Mcfarlane (9) — 13
- Polly Boyles (9) — 14
- Kathryn Jeanes (9) — 14
- Joseph McIntyre (9) — 15
- Poppy Happle (9) — 15
- Louisa Murray (10) — 16
- Lloyd Stobbart (9) — 16

Sophie Davis (9)	17
Ollie Searle (9)	17
Victoria Rose (9)	18
Emily Collins (9)	18
Holly Truscott (9)	19
Andrew McDonald (9)	19
Reece De Gruchy (9)	20
Adam Fitzgerald (9)	20
Thomas Eade (9)	21
Courtney Davies (9)	21
Luke Pickles (9)	22
Lewis Hope (9)	22
Karla Lambert (9)	23
Ashley Munn (9)	23
Chloe Jones (9)	24
Matthew Rowley (9)	24
Simon Spencer (8)	25
Stephanie Payne (9)	25
Charlie Logan (8)	25
Matthew Darnell (9)	26
Joseph Darnell (8)	26

Oakridge Junior School

Hannah Rawson (10)	26
Yasmine Chaffer (10)	27
Laura Walton (10)	27
Thomas Jeffery (10)	28
Alisha Fowler (7)	28
Lauren Buttle (10)	28
Josie Cook (10)	29
Natasha Mundembe (10)	29
Adele Smy (9)	30
Callum Latuske (10)	30
Amy Tennison (10)	31
Ben Peart (10)	31
Mikey Kay (10)	31
Andrew Stanton (10)	32
Luke Ward (10)	32
Joshua Brede (10)	32
Joe Hill (10)	32
Simone Ball (9)	33

Gemma Dutton (9)	33
Rachel Tarry (10)	34
Jordan Wilson (10)	34
Hannah White (10)	35
Ashley Cherrett (10)	35
Daniel Belton (10)	36
Phoebe Nielsen (8)	36
Kaisha Brown (10)	36
Jake Bills (10)	37
James Uysal (9)	37
Leah Nicholetts (10)	37
Thomas Tipler (10)	38
Jasmine Emery (10)	38
Holly Anderson (10)	39
Craig Oliver (11)	39
Hayleigh Moore (9)	40
Ryan Lacey (10)	40
Kelvin Hallett (10)	41
Matthew Harrington (10)	41

Park Gate Primary School

Jack Humphrys (7)	42
Jake Houghton (7)	42
Luke Holland (7)	43
Abbie Daniel (7)	43
Chloe Metcalfe (7)	43
Christie Bowers (8)	44
Chelsea Delaney (7)	44
Daniel Oliver (7)	45
Oliver Scott (7)	45
Thomas Silvester (7)	45
Kara Day (7)	46
Molly-May Keith (7)	46
Luke Jackson (7)	47
Molly Backhouse (7)	47
Carmen Lewis (7)	48
Kayleigh Louise Munn (7)	48
Thomas Doidge (7)	49
Emily Alexander (7)	49
Perry Collins (7)	49
Lloyd Coxall (7)	50

Jamie Young (7)	50
Abby Hartley (7)	51
Emma Welch (7)	51
Tilly Williams (7)	51
Lauren Bull (7)	52
David Roche (7)	52
Marcus McKellar (7)	52
Marcus Harrop (7)	53
Jack Bennett (7)	53
Oliver Metcalfe (7)	54
Katy Jelley (8)	54
Owen Brown (7)	55
Kate Laws (8)	55
Sasha Scott (8)	56
Maisie Hamilton (7)	56
Nicole Dollery (7)	57
Lily Lawrence (7)	57
Courtney Simmonds (7)	58

Rownhams St John's Primary School

Amy Garrod (10)	59
Becky Petley (10)	60
Eleanor Brander (9)	60
Hannah Williams (10)	61
William Jackson (10)	62
Vicky Nash (10)	62
Sophie Barrett (9)	63
Daniel Race (10)	64
Robert Warman-Johnston (10)	64
James Clark (9)	65
Jay Read (9)	65
Michael Stubbles (10)	66
Greg Facey (9)	66
Matthew Sandle (11)	66
Harriet Payler (10)	67
Jacob Godden (10)	67
Amy Neal (9)	68
Bradley Fletcher (10)	68
Abby Slater (10)	69
Sam Winter (10)	69

Samuel Smith (9)   70
Holly Scott (10)   70

Shipton Bellinger Primary School
Nathan Sykes (8)   70
Kate Smith (8)   71
Zak McMillan (8)   71
Victoria Charlton (8)   72
Jack Thomson (8)   72
Emily Dabill (8)   73
Amelia Taylor (8)   73
Molly Banting (8)   74
Max Shanley (8)   74
Billy Evans (8)   74
Heather Cullen (8)   75
Nicholas Phillips (9)   75
Lauren A'Lee (9)   76
Lauren Black (8)   76
Luke Hobson (8)   77
Georgia-Rose Sessions (8)   77
Francesca Worsley (8)   78
Kyle Hulse (8)   78
Evangeline Kitchener (9)   79

Shirley Junior School
Billie Davis (9)   79
Rebecca Peppiatt (9)   80
Simon Kian (9)   80
Nicholas Dobbs (9)   81
Tom Capper (9)   81
Caius Neale (9)   81
Kerry Gaul (10)   82
Robbie Smart (9)   82
Joshua Mills (9)   83
Katherine Evans (9)   83
Laura Paull (9)   83
Hayley Davis (9)   84
Ayanna Gadsden-Jeffers (10)   84
Wendy Smith (9)   85
Rosalynn Benyon (9)   85
Laura Loades (9)   86

Callum Ferguson (9)	86
Naomi Rides (10)	86
Lerryn Edghill (9)	87
Emily Harrison (9)	87
Paige Morgan-Giles (9)	88
Adam Thaxter (9)	88
Gabriella Catling (9)	89
Billy Granger (9)	89
Andrew Davies (9)	89
Daisy Haynes (9)	90
Stephen Peckham (10)	90
Aaron Bradley (9)	90

Sun Hill Junior School

Benedict Tilbury (9)	91
Kathryn Stokes (11)	91
Jake Sawyer (11)	92
Luke Marsden & Rhys Jones (10)	92
Megan Kempster (9)	93
Aiden Jones (9)	93
Benedict Tucker (10)	94
Savanna Paulsen-Forster (10)	94
Sophie Wilcox (11) & Stephanie Powell (10)	95
Peter Hurrell (9)	95
Katie Olbiks-Hill & Mollie Walters (10)	96
Abigail Pond (9)	96
Joe Dennehy (11) & Frainey Spurge (10)	97
Oliver Bevan (10)	97
Chelsea Green & Kirsty Hamlen (10)	98
Matthew Patrick (9)	98
Becky Page & Alice Burrows (10)	99
Naomi Barnett & Hayley Bennett (10)	99
Ethan Wesley (10)	100
Katie Fisher & Charlie Holmes (11)	100
Daniel Lowman (10)	101
Alex Dale (11) & Aaron Fisher (10)	101
Alex Penfold & Jamie Blanchard (10)	102
Charlotte Hurrell (9)	102
Susanna Diver (8)	103
Anna Sulston (9)	103
Olivia Probert (9)	104

William Dennehy (9)	104
Megan Lord (9)	105
Joshua Gates (8)	105
Jessica Arrowsmith (8)	106
Sophie Fairbairn (8)	106
Sharni Gibbs (9)	107
Madeline Quirk (9)	107
Brett Sawyer & Tom Hanks (8)	107
Jack Messenger (8)	108
Claire Matheson (9)	108
Haydn Jones (9)	108
Harry Nugent (9)	109
Harvey Watson (8)	109
Kaylie Grace (9)	109
Ashleigh Wilmot (10)	110
Makayla Bannister (9)	110
Peter Amey (8)	110
Celeste Richards (9)	111
Nicola Fry (9)	111
Alexander Dobner (8)	112
Naomi-Jane Andrews (10)	112
Emily Milburn (9)	113
Lewis Markwick (10)	113
Milo Ogus, Ashley Burnett & Matthew James (8)	113
Hettie Whale (9)	114
William Turner (10)	114
Liam Forcey (10)	114
Esther Southwick (10)	115
Alexander Arrowsmith (10)	115
Abbie Hughes & Nadia Hansford (8)	115
Nicholas Coles (10)	116
Calum Sheppard (9)	116
Nathan Humphrey (9)	116
Laura Hogg, Abigail Dailly & Chelsea Lane (10)	117
Matthew Waite & Stefan Clarkson (10)	117
Danielle Messer (8)	117
Jordan Pitter (10)	118
Sophie Carey (10)	118
Lucy Watson (8)	119
Megan Aynsley (8)	119
Thomas Brookes (8)	120
Zachariah Gilmore & James Page (8)	120

Frances Jarvis (8) — 120
Clodagh McSweeney (9) — 121
George Long & Bobby Matthews (10) — 121
Thomas Waite & James Timberlake (8) — 122
Rebecca Simpson & Emily Biehn (8) — 122
James Harrison & Samuel Wilson (8) — 122
Jenni Stokes, Emma Welford & Cassie Joss (8) — 123
Pascale Chalmers-Arnold (8) — 123
James Masters (8) — 123
Matthew Moss (9) — 124
Karl Stevens (8) — 124
Alec Thorne (9) — 125
Jessica Powell (8) — 125
Charlotte Wills (8) — 126
Aidan Pond (8) — 126
Toby Hartshorn (9) — 126
Jessica Blanchard (8) — 127
Ellie Grant (8) — 127
Peter Barnett (9) — 127
Rosalind Jones (9) — 128

Townhill Junior School
Becky Hart (10) — 128
Summer Fancett (9) — 129
Danielle Nixon (9) — 129
Clarese Winwood (7) — 130
Rebecca Quilter (11) — 130
Joseph Venable (9) — 131
Juanita Jordan (8) — 132
Julia Jordan (8) — 132
Jade McLean (10) — 133
Demi Naismith (8) — 133
Emily Dowling (10) — 133
Sarah Chun (10) — 134
Georgina Diffey (10) — 134
Kirsty Hunt (9) — 135
Milly Ann Mintram (7) — 135
Brodie Wheeler-Osman (9) — 136
Jasmin Urquhart (8) — 136
Katie Cluett (10) — 136
Ryan Hunt (8) — 137

Westbourne Primary School
David Harrold (9)   138
Charlotte Leach (9)   138
Matthew Cowen (9)   139
Ashley Airton (7)   139
Zak Conlon (9)   140

The Poems

What Is Brown?

What is brown?
A tree is brown
Lots of conkers on the ground.

What is yellow?
The sun is yellow
In the sky bright and mellow.

What is red?
Blood is red
Evil and dead.

What is white?
The moon is white
Sleeping in the night.

What is brown?
A tree is brown
It makes me frown.

What is black?
The night is black
There's no doubt about that.

How many colours can you see?

Megan Purkis (7)
Fryern Junior School

Colours

What is red?
The sun is red.
Make marshmallows
And go to bed.
What is green?
A bean is green.
What is white?
A light is white.

Yasmin Bradshaw (7)
Fryern Junior School

The Magic Box
(Based on 'Magic Box' by Kit Wright)

I will put in my box . . .
the glint of freshly polished metal,
the comfort of an armchair,
the roar of a brand new engine.

I will put in my box . . .
the warmth of the sun on sand,
the taste of warm food on a cold day,
the burst of colour when I was born.

My box is made from . . .
the richest steel on Earth,
and black and white polished marble,
but mainly well polished and well carved wood.

I shall glide in my box . . .
through the sky on a warm, soothing day,
on a tropical island where the sky is blue.

Shaun Moger (9)
Fryern Junior School

My Dad

The sound of the sea splashing against the rocks,
A bouncy rabbit,
A doughnut ready to explode full of sticky red jam,
He's a troll stomping around,
A dictionary looking for the right words,
He's the Eiffel Tower,
A pair of trousers walking about,
An eagle with food in its talons,
A tiger ready to pounce on its prey,
The sweet scent of a tulip,
A fast car zooming around.

Charley Cooper (9)
Fryern Junior School

My Magic Box
(Based on 'Magic Box' by Kit Wright)

I will spill in my box . . .
the dazzling rays of amber, blue and red of the sun,
the smell of a sizzling barbecue
and the echo of a cheerful Chinese cello.

I will put in my box . . .
the most bleak, shallow cough of a crestfallen cold,
and a dilapidated wrinkle of the most ancient face in the universe,
and the silhouette of an old rusty submarine.

My box is made from . . .
the finest silk of a summer's day sky,
with the truth of the world in the locks made of the biggest
                                              and roughest dragon scale,
and the lid made from petals of the most benevolent flower
                                                   of the Earth.

I shall lock in my box . . .
the bathing blue sky and the birds of paradise
and the sudden swish of the exquisite flames of the
                                            most considerate candle,
and the future, the future of my most marvellous life.

Lia Summers (9)
Fryern Junior School

My Brother

He's a monkey swinging in the trees,
He's an erupting volcano,
He's a banana, ripe and ready to eat,
He's an ice cream splattered on the ground,
A runaway train trembling along the track,
Squashed tomato down the lane,
A ripe, red apple dangling from the tree,
A fluffy cloud moving on,
He's a motorbike man.

Kevin West (9)
Fryern Junior School

My Magic Box
(Based on 'Magic Box' by Kit Wright)

I will put in the box . . .
the dripping red blood of an angry dinosaur,
the shiny stars from outer space,
the last book I ever read in my life.

My box is made from . . .
the red body of a dragon,
the very last coin I found in my pocket,
the dark sea of green and the bright blue sun.

I shall swim in my box . . .
across the wet, deep ocean floor,
a large blue lake to fill up my strength,
I will swim over the dark, black sun.

Mitchell Steele (9)
Fryern Junior School

What Is . . .

What is white?
The clouds are white
While the sun shines bright.

What is blue?
The sky is blue
While the mystery hunters hunt their clues.

What is red?
The sunset is red
While me and you go to bed.

What is grey?
The pavement is grey
Where I run to school every day.

Matthew Wenman (7)
Fryern Junior School

My Magic Box
(Based on 'Magic Box' by Kit Wright)

I will put in my box . . .
a blue frog jumping over poisonous parsnips,
the broom from an evil witch from a haunted house,
a tongue of a vicious two headed demon.

I will put in the box . . .
the kindness of a cheetah that runs faster than the wind,
a multicoloured sun from the cool, clear sky,
a singing sloth with six eyes.

My box is made from . . .
silky stuff with all sorts of big birds on it,
a dragon's skin with spiky scales,
a pig's nose snorting loudly.

I shall hide in my box
from a deadly monster from outer space,
the deep red Devil from underground
and a mummy from Egypt out of an old tomb.

Paige Edwards (9)
Fryern Junior School

My Nan

She's a fast dog.
A pair of glittering earrings.
The beaming sun.
A plate of boiling pasta.
She is a roaring lion.
She is a gazing little poppy.
She is a singing bird.
She is the moonlight.
A running waterfall.
She is a random romantic.
A piece of delicate glass.

Lauren Tarrant (10)
Fryern Junior School

Stars Up Above

A newborn star is very bright
As it sparkles in the night
A star is as bright
As a big flashlight.
In the night you can normally see stars
But in the day you cannot see stars
Even though they are still there.

Abbie Jackson (8)
Fryern Junior School

Stars

As shiny as a diamond
glistening in the sky.
Dancing in the sky
like little ballerinas
in a Christmas play.
The stars are twinkling bright
and moving around the moon
having lots of fun.

Olivia Stone (8)
Fryern Junior School

Wicked Witch

Witches are evil,
As deadly as poison.
They are a frightening sight.
Scary, mean, hairy, obscene.
Bad, sad, moody, rude.
Be afraid!

Katie Hodson (8)
Fryern Junior School

Me

I'm a dog barking in the night,
I'm a thunderstorm in the air,
I'm a monkey swinging on the tree,
I'm a teddy that you hug in the night,
I am an apple ready to drop,
I am a big banana waiting to be peeled,
I'm a runaway train,
I am a parrot flying in the air,
I am a planet in space,
I am a pizza with tomatoes on me,
I am a falcon flying round the sun.

Chad Mansergh (9)
Fryern Junior School

The Late Bus

The roses are red
But I am blue,
It's raining again,
The kids are singing their little song,
Because they're bored, they sing,
'Why are we waiting,
We are suffocating.'

Louise Giddings (8)
Fryern Junior School

I Am A Ruler

I am a ruler
I draw straight lines for all sorts of work.
I come in all different colours and sizes.
I love to have a nice home.

Emily Baker (8)
Fryern Junior School

Kind Beauty

I am a kind butterfly. I can fly.
I am really colourful and I have lots of patterns.
I love going on adventures and I love collecting
pollen from different flowers.
My name is Beauty.
I have loads of friends and they think that I am kind.

Ella Hannah (9)
Fryern Junior School

Ice Cream

Ice cream is tasty.
It is in all different flavours
Like strawberry and chocolate.
Flakes all over the place.
Ice cream dripping
All over the floor.

Kate Pile (8)
Fryern Junior School

The Ice Cream

Ice creams are delicious,
Yummy, yummy and yummy.
They make my thoughts cold
And me cold.

Kira Whitton (8)
Fryern Junior School

Munch - Haiku

Slowly, lazy, munch
and crunch all day, the crawly
caterpillars *munch!*

Daisy Trott (8)
Fryern Junior School

The Magic Box
(Based on 'Magic Box' by Kit Wright)

I will put in my box . . .
A rabbit hopping around,
A flower growing faster and faster all the time,
A photo of my family, but no one in it!

I will put in my box . . .
A giant foot,
A bit of a fairy's wing, winking at me,
Some fine wood, to remind me of my dream house!

My box is made of brown wood,
Coloured in with purple paint,
The lock, made from the hardest gold, golder than gold!

Eleanor Bowles (9)
Fryern Junior School

My People Poem

Snappy and soggy, with a bony back,
Roaring like a mad bull,
To relax while the sunset's coming down,
Playful people in Florida,
Big as a blow-up chair,
Listen to people running around,
Loves to eat sweets.

Sean Hopcroft (9)
Fryern Junior School

The Swan

I am a swan
I am as soft as a hamster.
I swim in the lakes and streams.
My wings help me swim
Because they push me back.

Sara Osborne (8)
Fryern Junior School

Me

I'm a golden retriever fetching a runaway ball,
A big bushy pillow with really soft covers around it,
I'm a tiny teddy bear always ready for a hug,
I'm the smell of Dove soap,
I'm a cute brown bear,
A cosy, warm bed no matter what,
I'm thunder and lightning heading your way,
A black volcano shooting out flames of fire,
A thin grain of rice,
A bulldozer knocking people over,
A bright red candle lighting up the room,
I'm a swing ball swinging around for my bed,
A girl dancing all the time.

Amy Allsop (9)
Fryern Junior School

Rabbits

I am a rabbit
who eats carrots
and grass,
I run around in the garden
like a cat.
I just love it.

Nadia Douglas (8)
Fryern Junior School

My Sister

My sister . . .
Has a memory of a wardrobe.
Kind as a dog.
A field of colourful corn.
Sound of a bird whistling.
Birds flying across a sunset.

Harry George (9)
Fryern Junior School

My Magic Box
(Based on 'Magic Box' by Kit Wright)

I will put in my box . . .
a trampoline to bounce me off to Europe,
the spark of an ancient fire, burning hot
and the day, month and year I was born.

I will put in my box . . .
my first baby tooth, the whitest it can be,
a drop of golden sand, slipping into heaps
and a stick insect jumping up and down.

My box is made from . . .
a smooth touch of silk shimmering with coloured glitter,
shining moons and stars twinkling down below,
and the scaly hinges are the fins from a baby fish.

I shall hide in my box
in the dark, secret, dusty corners,
then hide in a palm tree swaying in the breeze,
then whisk off to the black sun.

Lauren Harding (9)
Fryern Junior School

My Brother

My brother is a soft woolly jumper,
He's a sports car flashing past,
A bar of melting chocolate,
He's a roaring lion,
A rocky radio bursting with music,
My brother is a spice plant ready to grow,
He's a busy builder at work,
A shiny, coloured rainbow who glistens all day,
He's a roller coaster going round and round bends,
A pencil case, zipping itself up and down,
He's an angry patient waiting for treatment,
A dinosaur that steps on everyone.

Lucy Ransom (9)
Fryern Junior School

The Magic Box
(Based on 'Magic Box' by Kit Wright)

I will put in my box . . .
The first smirk from a baby.
An earring gun through my ears
As my eyes just turn hazy.

I will put in my box . . .
The first sight of Cornwall
And the first day at junior school.
The beach, the sea and the rocks
That was me.

My box is made from . . .
Glass, steel and gold that no one can hold.
The hinges are made from dinosaurs' fangs
And the key for the box, on the ceiling it hangs.

I shall bodyboard in my box
All in the sea with no one or nothing around me.
Just me and friends laughing and having fun,
Also riding dolphins and making new friends.

Kayleigh Gray (9)
Fryern Junior School

My Brother

He's a sesame seed waiting to grow,
He's a fast Ferrari speeding along the track at full speed,
A strike of ferocious thunder and lightning up in the sky,
He's the television always left on, on full volume,
He's a pizza slice waiting to drop the cheese dripping on the edge of it,
He's a torn piece of cloth trapped in a basket of feelings,
12 noon, the brightest and hottest part of the day,
He's an angry eagle swooping down on you with his sharp claws out.

Chloe Lebbern (9)
Fryern Junior School

The Magic Box
(Based on 'Magic Box' by Kit Wright)

I will put in my box . . .
an echoing voice running through an old train tunnel,
the breath of a fire-breathing dragon,
the blood dribbling off a witch's tongue.

I will put in my box . . .
the touch of rain splattering on my cold palm,
curly candyfloss swaying in the breeze,
a deep ocean octopus.

My box is made from . . .
bloodstained leather,
golden diamonds sparkling in the sun
with a cold metal handle.

I shall hide in my box . . .
from leeches in the deep pool
of deadly boiling lava,
from the erupting volcano.

Benjamin Limbrick (9)
Fryern Junior School

Baby Luke

He is a happy teddy
Waking up for his mum.
He's a bright sunflower awakening.
He's a statue, still and quiet.
A cute puppy ready to cuddle.
A bright, bouncy ball rolling on the bed.
He's a leaping frog ready to jump.
The tallest tower in the world,
Growing faster and faster.
A soft and colourful fur coat.
A monkey that is out of control.
A mixed up puzzle.

Faye Mcfarlane (9)
Fryern Junior School

The Magic Box
(Based on 'Magic Box' by Kit Wright)

I will put in my box . . .
the tender tale of an elm tree,
puzzles from Ancient Rome,
the sand spirit of a sunny southern shore.

I will put in my box . . .
nine robes of gold and ten of silver,
the last spark from an old fairy's wand
and the first feeble howl of a lion.

My box is made from . . .
soft silk of satin,
with gold moons and a silver lining,
it has huge hinges, as light as a feather.

I shall hide in my box . . .
away from the cries of sorrow,
to be comforted by a small furry kitten,
by a lovely, warm, cosy fire.

Polly Boyles (9)
Fryern Junior School

My Brother

He's a hedgehog with spiky hair,
A bouncy ball jumping around all day,
He's a dog barking all day long,
He's lightning ready to strike,
A fizzy drink ready to pop,
A monkey swinging about on some trees,
A zoo full of wild animals,
A motorbike zooming around,
He's a book talking on,
A computer full of ideas.

Kathryn Jeanes (9)
Fryern Junior School

My Magic Box
(Based on 'Magic Box' by Kit Wright)

I will put in my box . . .
Light blue flowers from the dark sun,
Some ducklings falling down from the air,
The noise of a fire engine.

I will put in my box . . .
My cat's sparkling eyes,
An egg of a seahorse,
The teeth of a shark.

I shall exercise in my box
I shall run in the wind,
I shall walk with my badger,
I shall hide from my ape.

Joseph McIntyre (9)
Fryern Junior School

My Magic Box
(Based on 'Magic Box' by Kit Wright)

I will put in my box . . .
a silver crystal glistening in the air,
a wand casting a spell over an evil demon,
a dragon with pointy horns.

My box is made from . . .
wolf skin,
with the shiny sea on top,
with the old fossils and a slithering, slimy jellyfish.

I shall jog in my box
to keep myself warm and dry,
with shaken wind and rain,
I shall do this to make me strong.

Poppy Happle (9)
Fryern Junior School

My Magic Box
(Based on 'Magic Box' by Kit Wright)

I will put in my box . . .
the sea swishing slowly through the raggedy rocks,
a heavy heart thumping,
a shadow of a bright silver elephant stomping.

I will put in my box . . .
a raincloud ready to open wide,
a green pea pod about to squirt glitter,
a cheetah climbing a black dusty chimney.

My box is made from . . .
gems, crystals, silver, gold and ruby red diamonds,
the last of the beautiful sky,
a heart full of love and singing blood.

I shall dream in my box
of the oceans with goldfish and octopus,
loving creatures with their hearts full of people
and how lovely they are.

Louisa Murray (10)
Fryern Junior School

My Dad

He's a ball of excitement just ready to pop,
A cloud of fun,
He's a tiger waiting to strike,
A flat drink gone fizzy,
He's an aeroplane ready to drop its load,
A bold banana split open,
A bird that can't open its wings,
A sports shoe ready to go,
A shining star,
A nut case that can't be opened,
He's a TNT bomb,
A wild thing.

Lloyd Stobbart (9)
Fryern Junior School

The Magic Box
(Based on 'Magic Box' by Kit Wright)

I will put in my box . . .
the photos of my friends and family
the gold at the end of a rainbow
the beam of the yellow sun.

I will put in my box . . .
a pogo stick that will go to space
the light from the stars
the moon from the universe.

My box is made of . . .
the magic from a fantastic machine,
the arms from a clock going backwards
the smell of pizza and a purr of a cat.

I shall add to my box . . .
the smell of a racing car as fast as the speed of light
the wings of a butterfly
ten petals from a daisy from Treasure Island.

Sophie Davis (9)
Fryern Junior School

Me

I'm a weird purring cat walking up a hill slowly,
I'm a crazy football player,
A monkey climbing up a tree madly,
I'm a long sausage eating myself up,
I am a fat hot air balloon ready to pop,
I am a dragon ride at an amusement park,
A bike pedalling madly up a hill,
I'm a computer louder than a foghorn,
I am faster than a number 5 train,
A football blasting up into the air.

Ollie Searle (9)
Fryern Junior School

My Magic Box
(Based on 'Magic Box' by Kit Wright)

I will put in my box . . .
Some shining salt water singing to the sky.
The voice of violent victims crying for help.
Some memories that whizz around my head.

I will put in my box . . .
The sound of sneaky stalkers
Peering through the windows of houses.
The heat of a burning piece of food ready to be eaten hungrily.

My box is made from . . .
The skin of a soft sheep,
The hinges are made of feet from a friendly lion
Helping people with difficulty.

I shall play in my box
Football and lots of other sports.
I shall also look back at my memories
To remind me about the good things in life.

Victoria Rose (9)
Fryern Junior School

Lucy Collins

She is the moonlight sparkling in the sky,
She's a crazy monkey swinging through the trees,
A bowling ball spinning around in the lane,
She's an ice cream melting in the sun,
The morning sun waking up,
She's the waterfall falling,
She's a cake being made in a shop,
She's a pizza with cheese being cooked,
A plant in the Eden Project,
She's a new tree growing,
A sea monkey needing to be fed.

Emily Collins (9)
Fryern Junior School

The Magic Box
(Based on 'Magic Box' by Kit Wright)

I will put in my box . . .
the shimmering shine of a cold star,
the mist of eyeballs,
a pair of smelly trainers, into the pot they go.

My box is made from . . .
slithery, slippery snakes' skin,
cobwebs so sticky it is impossible to break,
hardwearing gold that nobody could lift.

I shall do sports in my box
the marathon; hot, struggling through the heat,
football, my boots are the shiniest in the world,
cycling, madly moving to other lands.

Holly Truscott (9)
Fryern Junior School

Magic Box Poem
(Based on 'Magic Box' by Kit Wright)

I will put in my box . . .
My mum and dad when they laugh,
The smell of a roast dinner,
The smell of a fresh board pen.

My box is made from . . .
The golden leopard skin laid all over it,
Steel and a velvet lock
And snakeskin on the top of the box.

I shall put in my box . . .
The sound of a silent football pitch,
The snow when it's snowing hard.

Andrew McDonald (9)
Fryern Junior School

The Magic Box
(Based on 'Magic Box' by Kit Wright)

I shall put in my box . . .
the electric spark that can strike and blind the referees,
golden googly eyes,
the fold in footie goalposts, that have fans to direct
                              the ball away from goal,
the metal shin pads to injure their players.

I shall put in my box . . .
the spinning rugby ball that frightens their 9ft players,
the sinking monster truck sucked up from the sea.

My box is made from . . .
the layer of the rugby pitch that Wilkinson found his victory on,
the world's biggest pike all perked up,
skeletons and mummies as freaky as can get.

I shall wrestle in my box . . .
with Big Show and Eddie
easily thrashing Kurt and his assistant,
to Choke Slam his crippled manager.

Reece De Gruchy (9)
Fryern Junior School

Mr?

Hair is like a spiky chair,
Maybe a porcupine, but it's a he.
A Barcelona fan, his other favourite place is Rome.
An annoyed scream, like the squeak of a rusted droid
It is 12 o'clock when his belly rumbles,
Tick-tock, tick-tock.
A football-o-matic contestant,
Clever and cautious for swipes of fury with the ball.
The Eiffel Tower sometimes pushed to pencil point.

Adam Fitzgerald (9)
Fryern Junior School

My Magic Box
(Based on 'Magic Box' by Kit Wright)

I will put in my box . . .
The heat of a sausage on a dinner plate
The sound of the fresh air
The coldness of the white snow.

I will put in my box . . .
The taste of the Coke when it slides down my body
The sudden breeze that comes from the wind
The last word from my grandad.

My box is made from . . .
The chattering of rain on the roof
The running of the water when you have a bath
The rust of a metal pole.

I shall put a mixture in my box . . .
The feeling of the waves hitting you in the sea
The loud football crowd cheering, 'Goal!'
The thought of being celebrated in celebration assembly.

Thomas Eade (9)
Fryern Junior School

The Magic Box
(Based on 'Magic Box' by Kit Wright)

I will take my dog in my box
And I will put in my Game Boy to play with.
I will hear excitement,
Rocking on a roller coaster and water splashing.

My box is made from . . .
It is made of wood and plastic
And it has got pictures of dogs on the box.

I shall play in my box . . .
I shall take some games to play on, four in a row.
I will take some more games to play on.

Courtney Davies (9)
Fryern Junior School

The Magic Box
(Based on 'Magic Box' by Kit Wright)

I will put in my box . . .
the breath of a lazy lion,
a piece of cloud from the sacred sky (Heaven),
a tooth from a baby snow tiger,
the blade of a Chinese sword,
a ray from the gleaming sun,
a star shining in the midnight moon.

My box is made from . . .
the tip of a dinosaur rib for the hinges,
freshly cleaned silver for the locks,
9 carat for the decoration.

I shall have fun in my box . . .
like having barbecues,
having water fights and snowball fights.

Luke Pickles (9)
Fryern Junior School

My Magic Box
(Based on 'Magic Box' by Kit Wright)

I will put in my box . . .
my family in a picture in my box
and a shiny book which I have at home
and a old glitter plant in my bedroom.

My box is made from . . .
a piece of shiny wood for the handle
and the shine from a cow.

I shall put a skater in my box
with little wheels and glitter on the skateboard
and my little puppy.

Lewis Hope (9)
Fryern Junior School

The Magic Box
(Based on 'Magic Box' by Kit Wright)

I will put in my box . . .
The sound of the sea swaying in Spain.
The smell of pretzels being salted.
The feeling when I go on a roller coaster.

I will put in my box . . .
My very first word, repeating over and over.
The smell of Christmas dinner being served.
The nerves on the jumping bean.

My box is made from . . .
Gold and silver, bronze and happiness.
Treasure on the bottom and flowers on the top.
The hinges are made from the finest steel.

I shall dance in my box
All over the world from the breathtaking Atlantic
To sunny America on the scorching hot sand,
Then to India, in the burning summer.

Karla Lambert (9)
Fryern Junior School

People Poem

He springs like a chair.
He's an open door.
He shouts like a crazy monkey.
He's a python catching its prey.
He smells of men's aftershave.
He sounds like singing.
A dull morning in bed.
A pint of beer to end the day.
A magic man to make it a happy ending.

Ashley Munn (9)
Fryern Junior School

The Magic Box
(Based on 'Magic Box' by Kit Wright)

I will put in my box . . .
A feather from a soft swan in Spain.
The feeling of the roller coaster and the simulator.

I will put in my box . . .
The sound of the singing of a rock band,
Also the sound of the wedding bells for my aunty.
The sound of the arcade on holiday in Somerset.

My box is made from . . .
A gold shiny outside,
Swirly sequins on the top and bottom,
Around the sides are dogs and cats.

I shall put in my box . . .
A yellow beach with grey rocks around the side.
A yellow sun beaming at the sand.

Chloe Jones (9)
Fryern Junior School

Magic Box
(Based on 'Magic Box' by Kit Wright)

I will put in my box . . .
The second day of my life.
The first word I heard from my sister.
The first day I went to Fryern Junior School.

My box is made from . . .
The stars from the black sky.
With a lock golder than gold.
With a treasure of pleasures in every one of its corners.

I shall swim in my box
Inside the pitch-black waves of the sea.
Looking for all the gold
With all my Fryern Junior friends.

Matthew Rowley (9)
Fryern Junior School

Pepsi

Pepsi, oh Pepsi
Why are you fizzy?
Pepsi, oh Pepsi
It makes me dizzy.
Pepsi, oh Pepsi
Why are you fizzy?
Pepsi, oh Pepsi
I'm not dizzy.

Simon Spencer (8)
Fryern Junior School

People Poem

Snapping like an alligator.
Running down the stairs.
Always doing chores
And cheeky to his mum.
He always cheats in school.
He is a show off to his friends
And loves doing music.

Stephanie Payne (9)
Fryern Junior School

Traffic Light

When the red light is on
You need to stop.

When the yellow light is on
Get ready to go.

When the green light is on
You need to *go!*

Charlie Logan (8)
Fryern Junior School

Annoying Jo Jo

He is as hard as a metal table with red lumps.
He also stinks like a smelly, big fat chubby pig.
He lives where the smelly animals are living.
He barks like a little Jack Russell.
The time was 6.30 in the morning, and there were dark, black clouds.
He has green hair like grass which grows and gets cut off.
He shouts like a loud bell ringing.

Matthew Darnell (9)
Fryern Junior School

A Dog

A dog is louder than a boy,
Screaming like a girl.
Dogs are even faster than hamsters.
Not faster than a cheetah!

Joseph Darnell (8)
Fryern Junior School

Happiness

Happiness is yellow,
As bright as the sun.
A newborn baby's smile,
Great for everyone.

Happiness is celebrating,
All of those good times.
Bright pictures painted in my mind,
Birds chirping their chimes.

Happiness is comfort,
Surrounded by a bouncy pillow.
The prettiest flower of the bunch,
Is the soft and dainty willow.

Hannah Rawson (10)
Oakridge Junior School

Happiness

Happiness is a bumblebee
Collecting pollen from
A beautiful daffodil
In the summer.

It is waking up
On Christmas morning
And rushing down the stairs
To see if Santa has been.

Happiness is relaxing
On a Caribbean beach
With the palm trees
Swaying around you.

It is a chocolate bar
Always better
When shared
With a friend.

Yasmine Chaffer (10)
Oakridge Junior School

Happiness

Happiness is the colour yellow,
Everyone celebrating a happy new year,
People getting drunk and drinking lots of beer.

Happiness is the colour orange,
Everybody having fun in the depth of the pool,
Children playing under the bright yellow sun.

Happiness is the colour bright-green,
Kids opening presents covered in wrapping paper,
Laughing at a TV show called the Cartoon Caper.

Laura Walton (10)
Oakridge Junior School

Joy

Joy is a shield against fear,
A beautiful flower that protects you.
A smiling friend that is always at your side.
My back tingles,
I have a lovely feeling deep inside my stomach.

A snow leopard's stripy, soft, silky fur blowing in the wind,
Prowling through the mountains not a care in the world.
A beautiful white and black creature full of peace and joy.

Thomas Jeffery (10)
Oakridge Junior School

Apple

An apple feels slippery,
An apple looks red and shiny,
An apple smells sweet and fruity,
An apple tastes luscious.

Alisha Fowler (7)
Oakridge Junior School

Life

Life can bring anything,
Life is a baby's first cry, loud and sweet.
It is a baby bird learning to fly.

Life can repeat just like TV,
It can be sad or fun,
Surroundings changing and growing,
Different to everyone.

Lauren Buttle (10)
Oakridge Junior School

Happiness

Happiness is a dandelion,
Staring into the sky,
But when the flowers moults,
It has to say, 'Goodbye.'

Happiness is a friend,
Playing, having fun.
Children's faces all lit up,
Brighter than the sun.

Happiness is a moment,
When you wear a comforting smile.
It will help you in the future,
When you walk down the aisle.

Josie Cook (10)
Oakridge Junior School

Happiness

Happiness is the colour yellow,
Everyone celebrating a happy new year.
People dancing around
Like grizzly bears.

Happiness is the colour orange
Children having fun
At the depth of the sea
Adults sunbathing under the sun.

Happiness is the colour bright green
Kids opening presents covered in wrapping paper.
Laughing at the TV show
Called the Cartoon Caper.

Natasha Mundembe (10)
Oakridge Junior School

Peace

Peace is a plum
Juicy and sweet,
Soft on the outside
But squishy inside.

It is bubbles
Bubbling in a bath,
Frothy and foamy,
Warm and comforting.

Peace is a white rose,
Ready for anyone to sniff.
A sweet perfume
Encased in a flower.

It is a rainbow
Bright and happy.
The smile of God
In the clouds up above.

Peace is a snow-white dove,
Gliding through white, fluffy clouds.
It is silence
While other people fight at war.

Adele Smy (9)
Oakridge Junior School

Anger

Anger is a bull charging at a matador,
Horns ready to take him down.
Anger is a human, the red-hot fury bubbling up inside.

Anger is fire destroying everything in its path,
Anger is the Devil waiting to rise
Causing destruction in the land.

Callum Latuske (10)
Oakridge Junior School

Carelessness

Carelessness is the keys
Dropped down the drain.
The sad abandoned puppy
Left alone in the rain.
The felt-tip pens,
Left to dry with no lids.
The careless family,
Who won't admit what they did.

Amy Tennison (10)
Oakridge Junior School

Love

Love is a tingling feeling, happy and soft.
Love is a present, exciting and surprising.
Love is something that doesn't have a cost.
Love is a bank full of money ready to grasp.

Love is a peaceful happy life.
Love is a non-secret bond.
Love is a family life.
Love is a fun, joyful living way.

Ben Peart (10)
Oakridge Junior School

Fear

Fear is a monster under the bed,
A sheer drop on a roller coaster,
A jump over a waterfall,
A bungee jump from a balloon,
A murderer staring in at the window.

Mikey Kay (10)
Oakridge Junior School

The Sun

Beautiful golden yellow sun,
Your warming smile cheers up everyone.
Even on the coldest day
We like it when you come our way.
Your wonderful yellow light shines down on us,
Illuminating the world beneath you.

Andrew Stanton (10)
Oakridge Junior School

Horror

Horror is blackness and fire opening the gates of Hell.
It's demons and devils unleashed for death.
It is skeletons chained to the walls of dungeons,
It is zombies emerging from the graveyard of death.
It is a ghost hunting for his soul to reclaim it.

Luke Ward (10)
Oakridge Junior School

Joy

Joy is the colour yellow,
Joy is bright red like a tulip,
Joy is my mum,
Joy is happiness when I cuddle her.

Joshua Brede (10)
Oakridge Junior School

Anger

Anger is blood-red like a thorny rose,
A raised fist preparing to strike,
Opponents' eyes popping and veins ready to burst,
When my mum enforces her rules.

Joe Hill (10)
Oakridge Junior School

Friendship

Friendship is shaking hands,
with a new friend.
Friendship stands for,
love and peace.

It is a star,
rising in the sky.
It is a sweet
cottage pie.

Friendship is a heart,
never to break.
Friendship is love,
never to part.

It is a wishing star,
flying in the sky.
It is a colourful,
and loving bow tie.

Simone Ball (9)
Oakridge Junior School

Friendship

Friendship is a baby turtle
Left, then reunited with friends again
Swimming from his first breath
Following the current.

Friendship is sighs and secrets
Just between you and me.
Purple friendship pencil case,
Friendship is just you and me.

Gemma Dutton (9)
Oakridge Junior School

Summer

Summer walks
through the colourful fields,
leaving behind beautiful green trees.
She is a piece of blossom,
flying high in the sky.

Summer dances
by the glistening river,
Her long blonde hair brightens up the world,
She is getting the conkers ready to fall.

Summer creeps
into her hole leaving the world to groan
She takes her bright clothes deep down
and she is not to be found.

Rachel Tarry (10)
Oakridge Junior School

Jealousy!

I hate people who have good looks
and silky, clean hair.
It makes me really jealous.
People, children think they're so smart,
act smart, dress smart, but they're not.

It is really annoying when everyone
gets all the attention
and make comments while I'm talking.
People who are rich, all they do
is spend it on big houses and big cars.
That makes me really angry!

Jordan Wilson (10)
Oakridge Junior School

Spring

Spring tiptoes
Through the blossoming wood,
Touching trees when buds bloom;
Leaving trails of flowers and grass -
But never stops singing.

Spring whistles
By the foaming sea,
Planting each rock and stone
Skips through the blue ocean -
And then moves on.

Spring sprints
Down the rippling streams,
Catching at her breath
On her ankles were daisies,
At her back were little blue bells.

Hannah White (10)
Oakridge Junior School

Anger

Anger is a blazing fire
getting bigger and bigger inside you.

Anger is clenched fists
that will hurt someone.

Anger is ready to lash out
at anyone who it wants to.

Anger is a contagious disease
for which there is no cure.

Anger is a war of which
there is no stopping.

Ashley Cherrett (10)
Oakridge Junior School

Horror

Horror is black,
Death in a terrible way.

It is blood,
Trickling from clanking chains.

The smell of death
In a graveyard of mangled skeletons.

Demons and devils rising from
Dark gloomy churchyards.

Daniel Belton (10)
Oakridge Junior School

Apple

An apple tastes sweet and juicy,
An apple smells fragrant and fresh,
An apple feels smooth and slippery,
An apple looks like a shining red ruby!

Phoebe Nielsen (8)
Oakridge Junior School

Anger

Anger is a red apple sliced in half
Eyes popping out everywhere,
Veins bursting with fire,
Rules shouted in the house.

Anger is a tiger with an arched back,
Ready to pounce and release his claws.
A rhino with his head down
To show he's ready to charge.

Kaisha Brown (10)
Oakridge Junior School

Anger

Anger is blood-red like a thorny rose,
A raised fist preparing to strike,
Opponents' eyes popping out and veins bursting,
When my mum enforces her rules.

Tiger stripes are like thundering clouds,
An arched back ready to pounce
Released claws striking into its prey,
Fangs tearing the flesh of the carcass.

Jake Bills (10)
Oakridge Junior School

Summer Poem

The sun came out and showed his face,
His smile beaming all around,
His rays like arms reaching down,
Warming the people on the ground,
And as I looked into the sky
He breathed hot air down onto me.

James Uysal (9)
Oakridge Junior School

Hatred

Hatred is black,
So dark but so wrong.
It is fists, hot, sweaty and ready to punch.

Hatred is gritted teeth,
Too angry to speak.
It is your head aching with bad things.

Leah Nicholetts (10)
Oakridge Junior School

Happiness Is . . .

Happiness is a cloud
Drifting around.
Happiness is the colour yellow
Always brightening your life.

Happiness is a man
Free from his sorrows.
Happiness is a river
Powering the peace in the world.

Happiness is a bird
Breaking its boundaries.
Happiness is the trees
Whistling in the wind.

Thomas Tipler (10)
Oakridge Junior School

Death

Death is black,
All miserable and sin.
You'll feel so sad,
Unleash the sadness within.

Death is a pregnant lady,
She's had a wonderful marriage,
Now she's sad,
She had a miscarriage.

Death is unbearable,
So sad and glum.
Death is so rotten
Like a gone-off plum.

Jasmine Emery (10)
Oakridge Junior School

Summer

Summer sprints
Through the flowering wood
Swinging and turning,
Picking each flower with a peck
She whistles with the wind.

Summer danced
By the sparkling sea,
Skimming stones across the waves,
Climbing each rock lightly
And then moved on.

Summer tiptoed
Down the rippling stream
Following the ripples.
On her feet were sparkles,
Now she is fading into autumn.

Holly Anderson (10)
Oakridge Junior School

Love

Love is a pink heart,
A white feathered bird,
A white cloud in the light-blue sky,
A rainbow shining bright.

Love is a fledgling learning to fly,
Love is a child's first step,
Love is a baby's first word.

Love is a creamy chocolate bar,
Love is springtime,
Love is a baby lamb,
Love is kisses, hugs, romance, pink fluff.

Craig Oliver (11)
Oakridge Junior School

The Year Of Spring

Spring reborn,
The smell of beautiful flowers;
The lovely voice of a newborn lamb,
The cry of a fowl in the company of its brothers and sisters,
But most of all a baby in its mother's arms.

Spring returns,
The holiday of cheer;
The happiness all around us
A well-deserved award
And the meaning of life.

Spring glides,
Through the forest leaving bunches of flowers behind her.
Up and down the streams and rivers to sparkle the waters.
Around the clouds to brighten up the day
And in and out of the trees leaving bright leaves behind her.

Hayleigh Moore (9)
Oakridge Junior School

Anger

Anger is a fist clenched,
Blood all over the place,
Disobeying the rules.

Anger is a red face,
Anger is a devil,
Veins bursting everywhere
Up and down the stairs.

Anger is a dead person
Crying in a coffin,
Returning from the dead.

Ryan Lacey (10)
Oakridge Junior School

Winter

Winter prowls at every corner,
He waits to leap through the sky.
When he does, fog shoots from his body.
Ice is made when he gets mad,
He whips his vicious tail.

Winter leaps across the icy lake,
He loves the sound of people's cries.
The frozen river where people will play
But now nothing is left of autumn
Because it's dead.

Winter creeps from tree to tree,
Sending shivers from home to home.
Not love and affection but
Harsh pains of the cold
The green leaves are now dead and crisp.

Kelvin Hallett (10)
Oakridge Junior School

The Sun

The sun smiles down
And tickles the trees
Painting patterns as it moves.
Its happy face chases the clouds
And laughs away the rain.

The sun winks down
And dances through the fields
Making music as it goes.
Its warming arms cheer us all
And brighten every day.

Matthew Harrington (10)
Oakridge Junior School

Park Gate Sounds

At Park Gate I can hear . . .
children laughing.

At Park Gate I can hear . . .
noisy people.

At Park Gate I can hear . . .
lights switching on and off.

At Park Gate I can hear . . .
a noisy printer.

At Park Gate I can hear . . .
a door clanking loudly.

At Park Gate I can hear . . .
chairs clanking as they come out.

I like the sounds at Park Gate.

Jack Humphrys (7)
Park Gate Primary School

Park Gate Sounds

I can hear loads of gusts of wind outside.
I can hear lots of breeze and wind.
I can hear the doors slamming and creaking.
I can hear cars zooming past Park Gate.
I can hear the footsteps in the dinner hall.
I can hear people shouting on the field.
I can hear the clouds moving smoothly.
I can hear the computers going.
I can hear leaves falling softly from the sky.
To me Park Gate is fun.

Jake Houghton (7)
Park Gate Primary School

Park Gate Sounds

At Park Gate I can hear birds singing
and the people shouting
and computers printing.

At Park Gate you can hear people stamping
and a trumpet going like a horn
and a teacher blowing a whistle.

Park Gate sounds are good.

Luke Holland (7)
Park Gate Primary School

Park Gate Sounds

At Park Gate I can hear grasshoppers,
scratching their legs in the grass.
At Park Gate I can hear trumpets playing
and children chatting and shouting.
At Park Gate I can hear fans going on and off
and trees swaying to and fro.
At Park Gate I can hear doors banging
and metal gates screeching along the floor.
I love the sounds at Park Gate.

Abbie Daniel (7)
Park Gate Primary School

Park Gate Sounds

At Park Gate I can hear the sound of children playing happily.
At Park Gate I can hear a trumpet playing.
At Park Gate I can hear the humming fan in the ICT suite.
At Park Gate I can hear the distant sound of a motor blowing.
I love the sounds at Park Gate Primary School.

Chloe Metcalfe (7)
Park Gate Primary School

Park Gate Sounds

At Park Gate I can hear doors creaking and screeching
and a trumpet that is tooting loudly like a horn.

At Park Gate I can hear fans blowing like the breezy wind
and children chatting like squeaky birds.

At Park Gate I can hear doors banging open and closing
and lights clicking on and off.

At Park Gate I can hear chairs being bashed out
and wind swaying to and fro.

At Park Gate I can hear flowers emerging
and a gate scratching on the floor.

At Park Gate I can hear stones rustling and flies buzzing around.

At Park Gate I can hear trees swaying with the rustling leaves
and children stomping around.

At Park Gate I can hear clouds moving softly through the smooth sky.

I like the sounds at Park Gate.

Christie Bowers (8)
Park Gate Primary School

Park Gate Noises

I heard . . . the green giggling grass making a blowing noise.
I heard . . . the trumpets banging.
I heard . . . the wind making loud noises and the leaves being blown
                                                      by the wind.
I heard . . . lots of cars go *bbbrrrmmm!*
I heard . . . a bat, and a ball being banged by the bat.
I heard . . . stones being kicked.
I heard . . . rustling by the people.
I heard . . . wasps making a *bzzz* noise.
I like the noise.

Chelsea Delaney (7)
Park Gate Primary School

Park Gate Sounds

At Park Gate I can hear the wind and the trees swaying.
At Park Gate I can hear the rake making bumpy noises.
At Park Gate I can hear trumpets, they sound like an ambulance.
At Park Gate I can hear the dinner ladies getting ready for lunch.
At Park Gate I can hear stones rattling and children chatting
    like squawking birds.
At Park Gate I can hear paper making noises in the wind.
At Park Gate I can hear fans blowing and doors banging like drums.
At Park Gate I can hear the van's engine going softly.
To me Park Gate is fun.

Daniel Oliver (7)
Park Gate Primary School

Park Gate Sounds

At Park Gate I can hear . . . children playing and shouting in the
    home corner.
At Park Gate I can hear . . . the M27, cars roaring their engines to go
    fast on the motorway.
At Park Gate I can hear . . . 3AD's teacher blowing the whistle.
At Park Gate I can hear . . . grasshoppers rubbing their legs.
At Park gate it is fun.

Oliver Scott (7)
Park Gate Primary School

Sounds At Park Gate

It was so quiet at Park Gate that I heard
the wind blowing through the trees.
It was so quiet at Park Gate that I heard
a buzzing wasp flying.
It was so quiet at Park Gate that I heard
birds singing a lovely song.
This happened all day long.

Thomas Silvester (7)
Park Gate Primary School

Park Gate Sounds

At Park Gate I can hear computers flickering on and off
and doors opening and shutting.
At Park Gate I can hear a whistle being blown by a teacher.
At Park Gate I can hear metal dragging across the floor.
At Park Gate I can hear doors creaking and screeching
and paper blowing in the wind.
At Park Gate I can hear a trumpet being blown by a teacher or child
and grass being crunched and trodden on by children.
At Park Gate I can hear paper rustling through the photocopier
and children chatting like squawking birds.
At Park Gate I can hear children stamping their feet across the ground.
At Park Gate I can hear chairs being yanked out by dinner ladies
                                                        and children.
I like the sounds at Park Gate.

Kara Day (7)
Park Gate Primary School

Park Gate Sounds

I heard bees flying in the air like aeroplanes.
I heard crunching leaves fall from the bare trees.
I heard balls being kicked by boys on the field.
I heard teachers calling the children into the school.
I heard squirrels climbing up the trees.
I heard footsteps on the path heading to the classroom.
I heard eggs hatching in a nest in the tree.
I heard the wind blow the summer away.
I heard whispers of my friends in the line.
I heard a faint whistle from the playground.
I heard people breathing softly like a feather in the sky.
I heard all of these things.

Molly-May Keith (7)
Park Gate Primary School

Park Gate Sounds

At Park Gate I can hear . . .
the photocopier clicking and humming.

At Park Gate I can hear . . .
teachers shouting in the classroom, telling people what to do.

At Park Gate I can hear . . .
pencils scraping in the classrooms.

At Park Gate I can hear . . .
chairs rattling and scratching on the floor.

At Park Gate I can hear . . .
bikes and trikes making a noise.

At Park Gate I can hear . . .
children being very loud in the classroom.

To me Park Gate is fun.

Luke Jackson (7)
Park Gate Primary School

Sounds At Park Gate

It was so quiet that I heard a hammer bashing loudly against the wall.
It was so quiet that I heard the trees rustling very loudly.
It was so quiet that I heard the birds tweeting very loudly.
It was so quiet that I heard people splashing in the puddles.
It was so quiet at Park Gate that I heard a snail slithering across the playground.
It was so quiet that I heard the cars zooming past - *zoom, zoom.*
It was so quiet that I heard a trunk - *crack, crack.*
It was so quiet that I heard a crowd of ants marching towards me.
I love the sounds at Park Gate.

Molly Backhouse (7)
Park Gate Primary School

Park Gate Sounds

At Park Gate I can hear people talking as they put the chairs out
in the hall ready for lunch.

At Park Gate I can hear the wind buzzing past my ears.

At Park Gate I can hear the computers buzzing as they buzz like a bee.

At Park Gate I can hear the keyboards click like little mice
as their teeth go munching through their food.

At Park Gate I can hear the photocopier eating pieces of paper,
it makes a sound like a fire engine going *ne nor, ne nor.*

At Park Gate I can hear men kicking metal poles together
like clanking chairs, clanking against the table legs.

At Park Gate I can hear the engines of the two vans on the field
putting up the football goals.

I like the sounds at Park Gate.

Carmen Lewis (7)
Park Gate Primary School

Park Gate Sounds

At Park Gate I can hear people shouting like roaring tigers.
At Park Gate I can hear children laughing like hyenas.
At Park Gate I can hear children wiggling like fish.
At Park Gate I can hear people using their fingers to use the keyboard.
At Park Gate I can hear crickets making a crick crick sound,
and wind swishing through my ears.
At Park Gate I can hear lights going on and off,
and doors banging against the wall.
I like the sounds at Park Gate.

Kayleigh Louise Munn (7)
Park Gate Primary School

What I Can Hear At Park Gate

I can hear you.
I can hear people playing in the playground
and they are shouting very loudly.
I can hear the sounds of the green grass swishing.
I can hear people in the quiet area kicking the grass.
I can hear cars zooming past Park Gate Primary School.
I can hear the fast breeze brushing against my face.
I can hear *you!*

Thomas Doidge (7)
Park Gate Primary School

Sounds At Park Gate

It was so quiet that I heard my feet softly tapping against the ground.
It was so quiet that I heard the wind blow through the trees
and making leaves blow everywhere.
It was so quiet that I heard the orange fence scrape on the path.
It was so quiet that I heard the clouds gently sway through the sky.
It was so quiet that I heard the sun beam down onto Earth.
It was so quiet that I heard a bird's wings flap.
I love silent sounds at Park Gate.

Emily Alexander (7)
Park Gate Primary School

Park Gate Sounds

At Park Gate it is as quiet as possible, like a mouse.
At Park Gate it is as loud as a helicopter.
At Park Gate I can hear children laughing like mad.
At Park Gate I can hear the grass swishing in the breezy wind.
I like the sounds at Park Gate.

Perry Collins (7)
Park Gate Primary School

Park Gate Sounds

I can hear . . .
a trumpet like an ambulance.

I can hear . . .
Year 1 in the home corner.

I can hear . . .
the toilets flushing like a river.

I can hear . . .
the fan blowing in the breezy wind.

I can hear . . .
the teachers chatting to the children.

I can hear . . .
grasshoppers rubbing their legs.

Lloyd Coxall (7)
Park Gate Primary School

Sounds At Park Gate

It was so quiet at Park Gate that I heard
leaves running across the ground.

It was so quiet that I heard
teachers talking to their classes.

It was so quiet that I heard
trees swaying in the breeze.

It was so quiet that I heard
the dinner ladies cooking the dinners.

It was so quiet that I heard
the sound of pencils scratching.

Jamie Young (7)
Park Gate Primary School

Sounds At Park Gate

It was so quiet I heard a lonely snail slithering across the playground
                                      leaving behind a slimy trail.
It was so quiet I heard the leaves rustle against each other
making a rustle, rustle, rustle.
It was so quiet I heard the cars zooming past the school.
It was so quiet I heard worms making holes in the ground.
It was so quiet I heard feet stamping on the floor.
It was so quiet I heard spiders making their webs and having babies.

Abby Hartley (7)
Park Gate Primary School

Park Gate Sounds

The computer was noisy.
The wind pushed the leaves on the branches.
The leaves are noisy when they blow.
The children are noisy because they are playing outside.
Outside it is quiet.
In the quiet area the wind is blowing the leaves gently.
I can hear the wind in the air.
I like the sounds at Park Gate.

Emma Welch (7)
Park Gate Primary School

Sounds At Park Gate

It was so quiet that I heard leaves rustling in the tree.
It was so quiet that I heard teachers talking in the staff room.
It was so quiet that I heard teachers munching their lunch.
It was so quiet that I heard teachers marking children's work.
It was so quiet that I heard a petal falling off a flower.
It was so quiet that I heard my heart beating really fast.
I like Park Gate sounds.

Tilly Williams (7)
Park Gate Primary School

Sounds At Park Gate

It was so quiet that I heard
the moon in the night sky.

It was so quiet that I heard
the trees rustling in the wind.

It was so quiet that I heard
the water dripping off the trees.

It was so quiet that I heard
the stars twinkling in the night sky.

Lauren Bull (7)
Park Gate Primary School

It Was So Quiet At Park Gate

It was so quiet I could hear the scratching of the pencils in class.
It was so quiet I could hear the soft water dripping in the school pond,
It was so quiet at Park Gate I could hear the strong wind blowing,
It was so quiet I could hear the rustling of the trees in the playground,
It was so quiet I could hear the dried leaves crunching as the Year Rs
jumped on them,
It was so quiet in assembly I could hear the builders digging
up the field,
It was so quiet at Park Gate.

David Roche (7)
Park Gate Primary School

Park Gate Sounds

It was so quiet I could hear children shouting like angry gorillas.
It was so quiet I could hear the prickly breeze in the green grass.
It was so quiet I could hear a whistle like a bird.
It was so quiet I could hear lights clicking on and off.
It was so quiet I could hear the brushing wind.
It was so quiet I could hear a trumpet sounding like a horn.

Marcus McKellar (7)
Park Gate Primary School

Sounds At Park Gate

It was so quiet at Park Gate that I heard
People working sensibly.

It was so quiet that I heard
A small snail sliding on the playground.

It was so quiet that I heard
A plane flying in the sky.

It was so quiet that I heard
A car zooming on the road.

It was so quiet that I heard
The next door classroom.

It was so quiet that I heard
A door slamming shut.

It was so quiet that I heard
A rubber rubbing a pencil.

I like the sounds at Park Gate.

Marcus Harrop (7)
Park Gate Primary School

Sounds At Park Gate

It was so quiet at Park Gate that I heard
the car zooming.

It was so quiet at Park Gate that I heard
the bushes swishing with the wind.

It was so quiet at Park Gate that I heard
a cat miaowing.

Jack Bennett (7)
Park Gate Primary School

Silent Sounds

It was so quiet that I heard
a worm slithering across the playground.

It was so quiet that I heard
the wind rustling in my ear.

It was so quiet that I heard
the water in the drain.

It was so quiet that I heard
the photocopier buzzing.

It was so quiet that I heard
the laminator humming.

It was so quiet that I heard
the computer humming.

It was so quiet that I heard
the doors creaking.

Oliver Metcalfe (7)
Park Gate Primary School

Sounds At Park Gate

It was so quiet that I heard
the wind blow the leaves over in the playground.

It was so quiet that I heard
the leaves rustling in the trees.

It was so quiet that I heard
The crack of a branch as it snapped in two.

It was so quiet that I heard
a baby fly land on a beautiful bush.

It was so quiet that I heard
people walking around the school.

Katy Jelley (8)
Park Gate Primary School

Sounds At Park Gate

It was so quiet that I heard
a lonely slug slithering across the ground.

It was so quiet that I heard
scissors slashing.

It was so quiet that I heard
a fly marching across the ground.

It was so quiet that I heard
a leaf shaking off a branch.

It was so quiet that I heard
the wind push the door away.

It was so quiet that I heard
an ant walking across the ground.

The sounds are really good at Park Gate.

Owen Brown (7)
Park Gate Primary School

Sounds At Park Gate

It was so quiet at Park Gate that I heard
pencils writing up and down.
It was so quiet that I heard
a wasp buzzing busily next to me.
It was so quiet that I heard
a car zooming past.
It was so quiet that I heard
the grass stretching through the mud.
It was so quiet that I heard
raindrops dripping from the leaves.
It was so quiet that I heard
the clock going tick-tock.

Kate Laws (8)
Park Gate Primary School

Sounds Around Park Gate School

It was so quiet that I heard
a worm dig a hole.

It was so quiet that I heard
a fawn run into the trees.

It was so quiet that I heard
a fox run along the path.

It was so quiet that I heard
a leaf fall from a tree.

It was so quiet that I heard
a slug slithering along the path.

It was so quiet that I heard
a rabbit scamper into its burrow.

It was so quiet that I heard
a bird singing in a tree.

Sasha Scott (8)
Park Gate Primary School

Sounds At Park Gate

It was so quiet that I heard a bee collecting some pollen
and making his stinger wiggle.

It was so quiet that I heard something that was moving on the grass.
It was a big bird that was tweeting along the grass.

It was so quiet that I heard the dustbin clattering behind Park Gate
and it was really loud.

It was so quiet that I heard the trees rustling against the wind.

It was so quiet that I heard water whooshing around behind the gate.

Maisie Hamilton (7)
Park Gate Primary School

Sounds Round Park Gate School

It was so quiet at Park Gate School that I heard water dripping
from the leaves - drip drop, drip drop.
It was so quiet that I heard trees rustling in the wind - rustle, rustle.
It was so quiet that I heard bees buzzing gently round my head.
It was so quiet that I heard builders shovelling squidgy dirt
                                                                off the ground.
It was so quiet that I heard petals lightly falling off
                                      such beautiful flowers.
It was so quiet that I heard people splashing about,
but when people say shhh they all settle down.
It was so quiet that I heard birds singing on their lovely, soft branch.
It was so quiet that I heard wind contacting with my hair
                                                 to make it blow.

Nicole Dollery (7)
Park Gate Primary School

Sounds At Park Gate

It was so quiet at Park Gate that I heard
builders breaking bricks.

It was so quiet at Park Gate that I heard
flies zooming in the distance quietly.

It was so quiet at Park Gate that I heard
petals fall from the flower.

It was so quiet at Park Gate that I heard
a snail slither across the floor.

It was so quiet at Park Gate that I heard
water dripping down my back.

I love the sounds at Park Gate.

Lily Lawrence (7)
Park Gate Primary School

Sounds At Park Gate

It was so quiet at Park Gate that I heard
a door slamming shut.

It was so quiet at Park Gate that I heard
a tree whooshing in the wind.

It was so quiet at Park Gate that I heard
zooming cars.

It was so quiet at Park Gate that I heard
a lonely old snail slithering across the playground.

It was so quiet at Park Gate that I heard
little bluebirds tweeting.

It was so quiet at Park Gate that I heard
water d
    r
    i
    p
    p
    i
    n
    g off the leaves.

It was so quiet at Park Gate that I heard
bees buzzing around.

It was so quiet at Park Gate that I heard
the photocopier humming to itself.

It was so quiet at Park Gate that I heard
a big, scary spider.

I love the sounds at Park Gate.

Courtney Simmonds (7)
Park Gate Primary School

At The Bottom Of The Garden

At the bottom of my garden
There is such a surprise
My very own spaceship
Massive in size.

It goes to all planets
From Zarga to Zog
Laster and Macey
Pilla and Pog.

I meet many new friends
On my travels around
I name every planet
That I have found.

My best friend's an alien
With five thousand eyes
But blue coloured Martians
Are my favourite guys.

Some have spots or stripes
Some are green or blue
Some have tentacles
Some just go moo!

I have many adventures
When I'm bored or alone
I just zip down the garden
And go far from home.

You may think I'm strange
Or even quite mad
Though I might seem unhappy
I'm never ever sad.

Amy Garrod (10)
Rownhams St John's Primary School

My Family And Me

My house is made of trees
My garden is made out of fire
My next-door neighbour is a witch
My mother is a liar.

My mother is married to a monkey
Which happened to be my dad
They have a child which is me
They say I am mad.

I have five pets which are confused
My cat walks on one hand
As for my dog, she likes to eat
Every type of sand.

My rabbit is purple
My guinea pig is blue
My lizard is lovely
She looks like you.

This is my family
They're a little bit weird
Especially my sister
Who has a long beard.

Becky Petley (10)
Rownhams St John's Primary School

I Can See

I can see a pig wearing a yellow wig
I can see a snake eating a cherry cake
I can see a cat playing on a dance mat
I can see a dog floating on a log
I can see a bee . . .
Chasing after me!

Eleanor Brander (9)
Rownhams St John's Primary School

Please Santa Claus!

Please, please Santa Claus
bring me a puppy
with a tail and four paws.

Please, please Santa Claus
bring me a doll's house
with windows and doors.

Please, please Santa Claus
bring me a hamster
with a cage that it gnaws.

Please, please Santa Claus
bring me a brolly
to use when it pours.

Please, please Santa Claus
bring me a daddy
that never snores.

Please, please Santa Claus
bring me a mummy
that makes no laws.

Please, please Santa Claus
bring me a brother
with no trouble to cause.

Now Santa Claus I really must go
my dad's causing trouble
my brother's causing double
Ouch! Mum, you stood on my toe.

Hannah Williams (10)
Rownhams St John's Primary School

Hitler

In World War II he didn't know what to do,
He didn't even know how to eat stew.
He was on the run, he couldn't hide his bum,
Because he was very, very dumb.
He wore a funny hat, it looked just like a rat,
And he looked like Postman Pat.

In World War I he had a fat tum,
His mum had a fight and Hitler started to bite,
His mum got annoyed and took his ear,
The other fell off at the German pier.
She threw it out the window and it landed in the sea
And all the fish had his ear for tea.

When it came to marching, he couldn't command his troops,
He even tried to keep them in chicken coops.

William Jackson (10)
Rownhams St John's Primary School

I Wish I Was 4 Not 3!

I wish I was 4 not 3 because 4 looks better to me.
3 is too small and you're not trusted at all.
I wish I was 4 not 3.
I wish I was 5 not 4 because 5 is more alive.
I wish I was 5 not 4.
I wish I was 6 not 5 because 5 just is not alive.
So I wish I was 6 not 5.
I wish I was 7 not 6 because now I'm closer to 10.
So I want to be 7 not 6.
Now another 4 years go by.
Time just seems to fly.
Now I'm . . . 10.
But I want to start over again.

Vicky Nash (10)
Rownhams St John's Primary School

School

Drive a long way to get to the school
When we get there pay the taxi
Next we need to go into school
The teacher will need to take the register.

Line up for assembly
Ssshh! Walk in quietly
Sit down and don't talk
Listen to the teacher.

Next it's English, oh no!
The teacher is going on and on
About facts and opinions
Can life be any worse?

Walk out to playtime
Take out your snack
Apple, banana or cheese
No sweets!

The bell is ringing
The teacher announces
That next is science
Oh drat!

Now the fire bell rings
We all line up outside the smoke is rising
Hooray! We do not have to go to school
For one whole week!

Sophie Barrett (9)
Rownhams St John's Primary School

I Baked A Magic Pancake

I baked a magic pancake
And when it came alive
It ran across the floor
Doing the hand jive.

I baked a magic pancake
And guess what it looked like?
It had arms, legs, eyes and ears
It was just an amazing sight.

I baked a magic pancake
It ran off down the street
I had to try and catch it
Before it made someone shriek.

I caught the magic pancake
And it looked so yummy
I ate it for my supper
And it filled up my tummy.

Now there is no magic pancake
And it was such a shame
That I baked another one
And, uh oh, it's started again.

Daniel Race (10)
Rownhams St John's Primary School

Orange Is . . .

A brightly swimming goldfish in the sparkling water.
A golden orange tiger running through the jungle.
A shimmering crab walking through the water.
A shining starfish sitting on the seabed.

Robert Warman-Johnston (10)
Rownhams St John's Primary School

The Secret Of A Super Villain

In the morning he is a . . .
Fast talking
Fast walking
Cool kissing
Near missing
All knowing
Super villain
But at half-past eight he is a . . .
Thumb sucking
Mummy kissing
Cocoa drinking
Teddy hugger
Scaredy cat
Super villain!

James Clark (9)
Rownhams St John's Primary School

Football Crazy

Football is great
Football I will never hate
I love it to bits
I like wearing football kits
Football is fun
My friends say I'm number 1
I scored a goal with the help of my team
The other team are very keen
We work really hard so we can win
But sometimes we get kicked in the shin
I'm not lazy
I'm football crazy.

Jay Read (9)
Rownhams St John's Primary School

Speedy

My fishy is called Speedy,
He's 1 and a half years old.
My fishy is a goldfish,
He's small, fast, slim and old.

He has slimy skin,
He's as slimy as a frog.
Except he doesn't like to leap,
And he doesn't go on logs.

Michael Stubbles (10)
Rownhams St John's Primary School

Blue Is . . .

Blue is a sparkling blue sapphire
Blue is a thrashing, speeding dolphin
Blue is a rippling, crashing wave
Blue is a giant roaring whale
Blue is a great, shimmering colour
Blue is my favourite colour

What is yours?

Greg Facey (9)
Rownhams St John's Primary School

Rabbits

My rabbit is called Benson,
It is one and a half years old,
My rabbit is a dwarf highland,
It is grey and white.

Its skin feels of velvet,
And its ears stick up like a dwarf's,
Its tail is so, so tiny,
You can hardly see it.

Matthew Sandle (11)
Rownhams St John's Primary School

My Dog

Some dogs are sweet,
Some dogs are cuddly,
But my dog's the best,
Much, much better than the rest.

He doesn't like water,
And he loves milk,
Sometimes we even think he's a cat.

He's just like a little brother,
He even gives me kisses,
I could hug him all day,
The only problem is . . .
He's
Lazy,
Naughty,
Dopey,
Silly,
But very, very sweet.

Harriet Payler (10)
Rownhams St John's Primary School

Drip Drip

There was a boy called Danny Drip
But when he walks he just slips
All he does is drip drips
Out of the tap
He then lands up in the smelly sewer
Which takes about one hour to the sea
But he ends up being the only drop of fresh water in the sea
Then it happens all over again.

Jacob Godden (10)
Rownhams St John's Primary School

Lessons At School

Get a ruler,
Get a pencil,
Get ready for school.
Catch the bus, it leaves in five minutes time,
Drive far and far off to school.

Maths first, then literacy,
Oh no, here comes science,
Next it's ICT!

Line up for assembly,
Go into the hall,
Listen to the music playing while you're walking in.

Maths first, then literacy,
Oh no, here comes science,
Next it's ICT!

Walking to the kerb,
Across the road,
Getting on the bus to go.

Maths first, then literacy,
Oh no, here comes science,
Next it's ICT!

Amy Neal (9)
Rownhams St John's Primary School

Football

Football is a fun game, you will score some goals,
If you are Beckham you will score more than Scholes.

Beckham is a hero, his free kicks are class,
But in my free kicks I quite often pass.

In Beckham's free kicks he mostly shoots,
Because he has the most amazing boots.

Bradley Fletcher (10)
Rownhams St John's Primary School

You've Got Mixed Up!

'Can I have a ball for my birthday Mum?
Can I, please?
All I want is a ball, for me and my friends!'

'Okay, okay, stop nagging, I'll get it sorted.
I must tell your father!
You didn't give me much notice, it's tomorrow!'

'Your daughter wants a ball.'
'A ball!'
'Shall we get her a wool one?'

'Here you are, here's your birthday ball.'
'Already Mum, it's only 7.30.
How come it's wrapped up?'

'Just open it, hurry now!'
'Oh, it's a ball!
It's very soft and colourful!'

'Yes, just what you wanted, wasn't it?'
'No, no, no.
I meant a dancing ball!

You've got mixed up!'

Abby Slater (10)
Rownhams St John's Primary School

The Tramp

I know a tramp and he lives down the street,
He looks like a granny and he smells like feet,
He gets really drunk then he acts like a skunk.
The tramp won the lottery and now he collects pottery.
That tramp that used to live down the street,
He now is my grandad,
He doesn't look like a granny and he doesn't smell like feet.

Sam Winter (10)
Rownhams St John's Primary School

Rownhams Promotes Success

R ownhams promotes success
O rganisation
W orking hard to achieve in all we believe
N ever giving up when the going gets tough
H elping to care and share
A chieving our goals in all that we do
M aking sure we do our best to promote our
S uccess!

Samuel Smith (9)
Rownhams St John's Primary School

My Jack Russells

My Jack Russells
Are very cute
They're the best dogs ever
And they're extremely minute.

Their names are Lucy and Daisy
Sometimes they fight
But they love each other dearly
Trust me they don't bite!

Holly Scott (10)
Rownhams St John's Primary School

I Like . . .

I like the taste of sausage sandwiches in my mouth.
I like the smell of lavender when my mum burns it at night.
I like the feel of the metal on my army cars.
I like the sound of my air guitar CD, when I am riding my bike
                                                              in the garden.
I like the sight of fish when they are swimming.

Nathan Sykes (8)
Shipton Bellinger Primary School

My Cat

My cat plays
Jumps and pounces
Sleeps and leaps
Jiggles and bounces.

My cat purrs
Leaps and hops
Bounces and jumps
Sleeps and flops.

My cat squiggles
Curls and jiggles
Leaps and twirls
Plays and wiggles.

My cat leaps
Wiggles and curls
Tickles and jiggles
Wriggles and twirls.

My cat flinches
Twitches and licks
Squiggles and curls
Twirls and tricks.

Kate Smith (8)
Shipton Bellinger Primary School

Cats

White cats are soft,
Black cats are rough,
Ginger cats are lazy,
Tortoise shells are messy.

Zak McMillan (8)
Shipton Bellinger Primary School

Cat

The black cat growls,
Opens her jaws,
Stretches her legs
And flexes her claws.
Then she walks
And sits down on her long stiff legs
And walks some more.
She shows her sharp teeth,
She moves her lip,
Her slice of a tongue,
Touches her tip,
Licks herself.
On her delicate toes
She stretches her back,
As high as it goes.
She puts herself down
With particular care.
Then strolls away
With her tail in the air.

Victoria Charlton (8)
Shipton Bellinger Primary School

The Angry Cat

The angry cat scratches.
Bites and creeps.
Bounces and pounces.
Howls and miaows.
Spits and snarls.
Sneers and creeps.
Growled and hissed.
He is sly and never shy.

Jack Thomson (8)
Shipton Bellinger Primary School

Animals

Bunnies jump,
Bunnies pounce,
Bunnies scratch,
Bunnies bounce.

Horses neigh,
Horses clop,
Horses play,
Horses hop.

Cats scratch,
Cats bite,
Cats purr,
Cats fight.

Dogs munch,
Dogs bark,
Dogs scare,
Dogs spark.

Emily Dabill (8)
Shipton Bellinger Primary School

Cats

Cats scratch,
Cats bite,
Cats wake
You in
The night.

Cats purr,
Cats bounce,
Kittens pounce
On you
All night.

Amelia Taylor (8)
Shipton Bellinger Primary School

Dogs And Cats

Dogs chase,
Cats pounce,

Dogs bark,
Cats bite,

Dogs lick,
Cats purr,

Dogs leap,
Cats bounce.

Molly Banting (8)
Shipton Bellinger Primary School

I Have A Cat

I have a cat
That's very fat
And it's only 1.
It hates dogs and
Certainly frogs.
It went through the flap
For a cat
And saw a rat.

Max Shanley (8)
Shipton Bellinger Primary School

I Like . . .

I like the taste of bacon, salty on my tongue.
I like the smell of sausages, sizzling in the pan.
I like the feel of juicy oranges squirting in my mouth.
I like the sound of bells ringing in my ear.
I like the sight of the beach floating in the water.

Billy Evans (8)
Shipton Bellinger Primary School

Fun! Fun! Fun!

Beach, beach, beach,
Bury! Bury! Bury!
'Let's go and catch a ferry.'
Ice cream, ice cream, ice cream!

Yes! Yes! Yes!
'Oh what a mess.'
Sea, sea, sea,
Hee! Hee! Hee!
'Quick follow me!'

'Home, home, home.'
'No! No! No!'
'Come on let's go!'
'But Mum . . .

We're having so much fun.'
Fine, fine, fine,
Mine! Mine! Mine!
'No it's my turn!'
'No, it's my turn!'

'Right come on!
Home now!'

Heather Cullen (8)
Shipton Bellinger Primary School

I Like . . .

I like the taste of cooked breakfast tingling on my tongue.
I like the smell of crispy, crunchy bacon.
I like the feel of crunchy, crushed apples.
I like the sound of chirping birds.
I like the sight of a new game.

Nicholas Phillips (9)
Shipton Bellinger Primary School

The Cat Hunter

The cat hunter's mean,
The cat hunter's mad,
The cat hunter's really tall,
Though inside she's really sad.

She's already got tabbies,
She's already got gingers,
She wants some blacks,
Though she's got a cabin full of wingers.

Deep into the cabin,
Where everyone's asleep,
Hear the fire alarm,
Bleep, bleep, bleep.

Why I have the curse,
Why you're hating me,
Why I can't really know,
But soon you'll have to see.

I'm going to catch a boat,
And sail away to France.
Pull my curse away and leave the cats behind,
So I can dance.

Lauren A'Lee (9)
Shipton Bellinger Primary School

Splish Splash

Splish splash, I'm in the bath.
Splish splash, I'm getting washed.
Splosh splish, I'm being a fish.
Splash splosh, I'm being posh.

Clip clop, I'm going to hop.
Clop clip, I've hurt my hip.
Clap clap, I've got the sack.
What a hard day at work.

Lauren Black (8)
Shipton Bellinger Primary School

Pussy Cat Pussy Cat

'Pussy cat, pussy cat,
Purring around.
Where did you go?'
'I went up a tree
So that no dog could catch me.'

'Pussy cat, pussy cat,
Looking so good.'
'I'm going to catch a rat
Right now!
I am so bored sitting around.'

'Pussy cat, pussy cat,
So lazy.'
'I have a snoring appetite
So don't wake me up
For about three weeks!'

Luke Hobson (8)
Shipton Bellinger Primary School

Animals

Dolphins dance through the waves,
Babies splashing in the sea,
Fish flipping out of the sea.

Rabbits hop about,
Hamsters flop around,
Guinea pigs prance and dance,
Cats scratch things like the sofa.

Siamese sulk,
Tabbies play tag.

Sheep dogs sing by barking,
Greyhounds growl and howl,
Springer spaniels scratch.

Georgia-Rose Sessions (8)
Shipton Bellinger Primary School

I Like . . .

I like the taste of . . .
Fish and chips
Filling up my mouth.

I like the sound of . . .
Crunching leaves
Echoing in my ears.

I like the feel of . . .
Silk running
Through my fingers.

I like the look of . . .
Dolphins
Jumping in the water.

I like the smell of . . .
Crunchy bacon
Marching up my nose.

Francesca Worsley (8)
Shipton Bellinger Primary School

The Cat

The cat miaows,
Creeps down the stairs,
Hisses and spits,
Howls and miaows
And then goes out the cat flap.
Pounces and bounces
And then leaps.
Scratches and bites,
Growls, purrs
And snoozes to sleep.

Kyle Hulse (8)
Shipton Bellinger Primary School

Dogs

I love my dog, she is so, so cute
she's the cutest dog I have ever known.
I love her so dearly
as she sits on her throne.

Evangeline Kitchener (9)
Shipton Bellinger Primary School

Excitement

All around puppies yapping,
In the wind paper flapping.
Fire rising,
Waterfall crashing.
Animation surrounds me.

Dolphins leap, dolphins glide
Bubbles float, the waves they ride.
Smoky fire,
Pine trees,
Delirium bubbles.

Whizzing through space,
Twinkling rocket race.
Salty sea,
Hot spice,
Intensity burns up.

My body just can't stop,
I feel like I could pop.
One, two,
Three, four.
Discomposure reveals.

Billie Davis (9)
Shirley Junior School

Petrified

Petrified, the ghosts and ghouls,
Loud screaming in my ear,
Murderers stabbing in the night,
Wailing mothers I can hear.

Fists and boots slapping and punching
Gambling men put up a fight.
Piercing blood, the sour taste,
On this dark and gloomy night.

It's morning now, the sun has risen.
Rotten flesh smell fills the air.
You wake up and you realise now,
The blood stains in your greasy hair.

Rebecca Peppiatt (9)
Shirley Junior School

Mad!

Mad is like burning chillies,
Makes you full of rage.
Like your head will blow up,
A lion in no cage.

The feeling of burning coal,
The taste of lemon and lime.
Makes you feel so fuming,
A hedgehog in your spine.

Mad makes your face go red,
Your muscles start to tense.
But if you get too mad,
You'll get too incensed.

Simon Kian (9)
Shirley Junior School

Happy

Happy is a cool summer's morning,
Makes you feel so gay.
A pot of sweet scented pink roses,
Smiling every day.

Birds are singing cheerfully,
Faces lighting up.
Trees are barking happily,
Like energetic pups.

Nicholas Dobbs (9)
Shirley Junior School

Energetic

Energetic is a jaguar,
Twisting through the trees,
Active smells like Ferrari flames,
Brisk like a big cheetah.

Idle is like pouring lava,
A blur zooming past,
Strenuous footsteps coming and going,
Never stopping to take a break.

Tom Capper (9)
Shirley Junior School

Anger

Anger is a million spiders,
Spiky, burning grass.
A shark bite of bitterness,
Opaque and fiery glass.

Anger is a ball of fire,
Letting out fury, rage.
Your face is turning red,
This is fire in a cage.

Caius Neale (9)
Shirley Junior School

Calmness

Calmness is like a bed of feathers,
Floating through the air.
Calmness is the soft play of music,
But are you really there?

Calmness is the sea,
Sweeping upon your legs.
Calmness is the fresh air,
Brushing past your face.

Calmness is relaxing,
Like sand on the tips of your toes.
Calmness is so peaceful,
Like a smiling rose.

Calmness is like a trickling lake,
Where nature goes to drink.
Calmness is sweet candyfloss,
All fluffy and pink.

Kerry Gaul (10)
Shirley Junior School

Playful

Playful, smiling faces
Puckish children joking
White chocolate melting
In the boiling sun

Active children running
Crossing the finish line
Children eating sweets
And gingerbread men.

Robbie Smart (9)
Shirley Junior School

Boredom

Boredom is an empty room,
With nothing but a chair,
A place where no flowers bloom,
A gloomy dragon's lair.

TV gone, no one in,
Not even a little toy,
Dinner's yuck, booked for the bin,
My pirate ship's gone, ahoy.

Joshua Mills (9)
Shirley Junior School

Peace

Peace is pale like puffy clouds,
Drifting in a gentle breeze.
Peace is like birds singing,
In beautiful blossom trees.

Peace is wavy, bright green grass,
Peace is country air.
Peace is a soothing wind,
Wisping through your hair.

Katherine Evans (9)
Shirley Junior School

Joy

Perching on the trees are robins in the sun,
Children sitting on the grass watching rabbits run.

Gleeful mums and dads are talking with a cup of tea,
People having picnics overlooking the greeny sea.

Happy sailors in their boats going to the bay,
All the children go to bed ready for the next bright day.

Laura Paull (9)
Shirley Junior School

Anger

Anger is like a fire consuming everything in its way.
Anger is like a great earthquake ripping up the Earth.
Anger is like a plaster of fire stuck around you.
Anger is like burning hot water on the tip of your tongue.
Anger is like hot air letting off masses of steam.
Anger is annoyance, irritation, displeasure, resentment, rage and fury
Mixed together in your head.

Anger is a drape of blackness covering everything up.
Anger is like a bomb blowing up the world.
Anger is like carbon dioxide suffocating you.
Anger is like strong lemon bitterness in your mouth.
Anger is like burning wood smoke trailing off.
Anger is annoyance, irritation, displeasure, resentment, rage and fury
Mixed together in your head.

Hayley Davis (9)
Shirley Junior School

Shocked

Shocked!
A monster jumping out at you.
The sour taste of lemon juice.
The sudden stream of haunting ghosts
An alarm clock going off.

The alarming sound of the fire drill
The brightness of the sun
The burning shock of an electric wire
Your hair sticks up - so stunned!

Ayanna Gadsden-Jeffers (10)
Shirley Junior School

Timid

Timid is manky mango and melon,
Poison from a snake,
And your best friend being choked
And a slice of devil cake!

Disgusting diesel
Pet being hurt,
Fresh onions
And you being caught!

Timid is unadventurous
And very diffident
Mousy, shrinking and afraid
My face is red, I'm so scared!

Yucky! Yucky!
Tomatoes yuck!
Sheepish and shy
Very bad luck.

Wendy Smith (9)
Shirley Junior School

Furious

Fury is violent waves
Like icicles of fire
A bed of lava
Raging, savage, mild.

Inside I am boiled
Enraged and fuming
Ghostly faces scream
Livid, mad, wrathful.

Rosalynn Benyon (9)
Shirley Junior School

Sadness

Sadness is a ball of tears,
Travelling with you through the years.
A tragic moment in your life,
It hits you like a burning knife.

Sadness runs through your blood,
Bursting out like a flood.
It makes you upset and very mad,
Which makes you do things that are bad.

Laura Loades (9)
Shirley Junior School

Anger

Anger is a fiery bandit screaming all day long,
Giant monsters hitting you with hard clubs.
Volcanoes erupting all day in the sun,
Bunnies burning all night they're gone.

Anger is pure red blood everywhere,
Hordes of stinging mosquitoes stinging your arm.
Raging children shouting in the sun,
Feeling the pain in the hot, hot sun.

Callum Ferguson (9)
Shirley Junior School

Deserted

I feel as if I'm sitting in mid-air
I see emptiness and air all around me
I feel alone and hated in every single way
Like my soul has just been taken away

I feel betrayed and desolate
All I taste is long lost chocolate
Melting away in my mouth
All I smell is cigarette smoke.

Naomi Rides (10)
Shirley Junior School

Fury

Stomping, romping, up the stairs,
Slam the door without a care.

A ball of fire in front of your eyes,
Bloodcurdling screams, shouts and cries.

A tempest sea banging on the rocks,
Against the side of the cliffs it knocks.

Standing barefooted on a bed of pins,
A scorpion pinch on your leg that stings.

Rotten fish annoying your tongue,
Flaming hot chilli that burns like the sun.

Smoke from a raging forest fire,
Rising up through the trees even higher.

Lerryn Edghill (9)
Shirley Junior School

Bored

Boredom is like a dreary hole
Dry and flat
Dull and blank
Humdrum and long winded

Boredom is like burning olives
Emotions run wild
Teardrops fall
Cold and weak

Boredom is like one hundred ice cubes
And the coldness increases on your tongue
And then you fall into a deep sleep.

Emily Harrison (9)
Shirley Junior School

Anger

Anger is apoplectic
A burning ball of rage
That makes you go hectic
Like you're locked up in a cage.

Anger is swallowing swords
That makes your face go red.
The gruesome death of the lords
When the sacrifice is fled.

Anger is a lava bed
Travelling through your veins.
Awaking the dead
Clanking at their chains.

Paige Morgan-Giles (9)
Shirley Junior School

Shyness

A deserted village
Everyone's indoors
A mouse looking for cheese
On the very dusty floors

A mousy, bashful girl
Looking at the ground
A moon-pale face
Making no sound

A boy full of shyness
Fearing everyone
Shaking his feet
Scared of having fun.

Adam Thaxter (9)
Shirley Junior School

Fury

Fury is a ball of fire
And I can't let go.
It's like a sea urchin sting,
Without that sea to flow.

Fury is violent, deadly,
Anything else bad.
Burning on lava,
I'm red-hot and dead.

Its flames burning all around,
Like a bonfire,
My body inside is flaming,
Like overcooked chilli.

Gabriella Catling (9)
Shirley Junior School

Happy

Happy is an ice cream melting in your mouth
Having your favourite meal and eating it yourself.

Happy is a holiday, let's go and have a swim,
We can dive and play and splash, I've just banged my chin.

Billy Granger (9)
Shirley Junior School

Happiness

Happiness is caterpillars on your arms,
The relief of no fire alarms.
Like soft fur and a cat's purr.
Like waves crashing on the beaches
And schools with no teachers.

Andrew Davies (9)
Shirley Junior School

Anger

Anger is a burning oven
Swords of flaming fire,
A ball of burning irritation
Your temper goes higher and higher.

Fury is a burning chilli
The roar of a lion,
The smoky smell of a cigar
The burn of an iron.

Daisy Haynes (9)
Shirley Junior School

Livid

Livid is a ball of rage,
Smelling like fire,
Of an old lit cigarette,
Raging at a liar.

Livid is annoying children,
Messing up your room,
Livid is a bed of lava,
Boiling till your doom.

Stephen Peckham (10)
Shirley Junior School

Fury Poem

Fury's like a tongue of flame
Like a bomb exploding,
Looks like a lava flow
Smells like a volcano

Fury's like a supernova
A livid ball of rage,
Like a rocket taking off
A wrathful knife of fire.

Aaron Bradley (9)
Shirley Junior School

Puddle Jumping

P itter-patter goes the rain
U nder is us, jumping through it, jumping in it
D ips in the ground hold water
D ips in the ground make puddles
L et the puddles fill, fill, overflow
E ven the adults play in the water

J umping, splashing
U nlimited fun
M um is mumbling, 'Where is the sun?'
P erhaps one day she will learn that the rain is great
I s it true that people hate the rain?
N othing is better. One day people should learn that the rain is fun
G rinning faces, happy lives, water makes the world spin.

Benedict Tilbury (9)
Sun Hill Junior School

Super Dog

Super Dog is my name
Undoing wrongs is my game
Puppy power, incredible strength
One metre fifty is my length
Saving dogs is what I do
When you need saving I'll be there for you.

Running down the corridor
No one can trip *me* on the floor
Everyone can stop me being tough
But when I'm here I'm really rough
Super Dog is my name
Undoing wrongs is my game.

Kathryn Stokes (11)
Sun Hill Junior School

Ruff The Super Dog, The Super Hog And Super Frog

Ruff the super dog is a loopy dog
He flies down the alleyway to the bog
He zooms to the pond to save a frog
He is a cool dog but not as good as Super Frog.

Super frog is a cool frog
He also lives under a log
He jumps from lily pad to lily pad
He flies to his dad
He is friends with Super Dog
But not with Super Hog.

Super hog is a pooper hog
He can pick up Super Frog's log
But then he sees
A quite big swarm of bees.

Jake Sawyer (11)
Sun Hill Junior School

Spider-Man

S caling walls, up he climbs
P ulverising crime with his web-flying skills
I nvincible he stays after every crime he slays
D efeats all the villains that try to get away
E verlasting enemies Spider-Man will have
R ed and blue are the colours of his suit

M ercy the villains cry
A s Spider-Man ties them in his unbreakable web
N ow he swings through the city's streets always claiming victory

Luke Marsden & Rhys Jones (10)
Sun Hill Junior School

Yesterday Today

Yesterday
Yesterday was brighter than a light bulb
Hotter than a desert, clouds just drifting by,
No wind in the air.
A shimmering sunshine overhead
Everyone was too hot to work
No one was bothered to even walk and then it rained

Today
Today is wet and dull; wetter than a river,
But now it's clearing all away,
I hope it's going to be a brighter day.
Brighter than yesterday, brighter than a desert,
Hotter than a bath, wildlife in the sky.
Not the same as today, no sounds in the air.

Megan Kempster (9)
Sun Hill Junior School

Puddle Jumping

P uddles are fun
U nusual things the puddles are like
D oodles on a piece of paper you
D on't know what they are going to turn out
L ike, they are dirty almost
E very day

J umping in the
U nique
M assive
P uddles
I will
N ever stop until it is time to
G o in.

Aiden Jones (9)
Sun Hill Junior School

The Battle Of Arthur Itis And Mr Ree

Arthur Itis with his crones,
Severed Sam and Broken Bones.
Once attacked Mr Ree,
Right in daylight, plain to see.
Mr Ree using the forces of good,
Put on his cloak with a shiny hood.
And changed his name very slightly,
To mystery and very mightily.
Ran at quite a tremendous speed,
And Severed Sam turned and fled.
Then Arthur Itis turned his torso
And then he turned it even more so.
Then what should come out of his belly,
But a liquid that turned him into jelly.
And so that was the end of Old Mystery,
But Arthur and Bones turned to see
A quite gigantic living ted
And the teddy hugged so much that Itis and Bones
Are now quite dead.

Benedict Tucker (10)
Sun Hill Junior School

Super Daisy

My name is Super Daisy
I can be a little lazy
When you are in trouble
I turn into a double daisy

My name is Super Daisy
I can be a little lazy
I run down the hall
And up the wall

I can save you all.

Savanna Paulsen-Forster (10)
Sun Hill Junior School

I Am Now A Superhero

One day I said to Mr Truo,
'I am now a Superhero.'
Then I said, 'I'm on a mission,
Bob is on the loose with a piston.'

My name is Rescue Boy
And my shotgun's not a toy.
Bob will be behind bars,
While I'm driving soft-top cars.

I found him in the Dairy Bar,
Ordering a strawberry tart.
Hands up I say,
Or you will pay.

Now I'm in detention,
Just because he had to mention.
Exactly how I broke his arm,
While the office told my mam.

Sophie Wilcox (11) & Stephanie Powell (10)
Sun Hill Junior School

The Feeling Of The Wind

The wind rustles leaves up in the trees
'What is that noise?' I ask my father.
'That is the wind, the wind is like a monkey
Climbing trees,' he answered.
The wind throws leaves along the ground
'What is that noise?' I ask my father.
'That is the wind, the wind is like a gazelle
Running along the ground,' he answered.
The wind rushes.
'What is that feeling?' I ask my father.
'That is the feeling of the wind.'

Peter Hurrell (9)
Sun Hill Junior School

I Am A Superhero

I am a superhero,
a superhero am I.
I sprint the roofs and climb them
and can jump extremely high.
I am a superhero,
a superhero am I.
I save a lot of people
and have an X-ray eye.
I am a superhero,
a superhero am I.
I come as quick as I can
and defeat the bad guy.
I am a superhero,
a superhero am I.
I try and make you happy,
instead of making you cry.
I am a superhero,
a superhero am I.
I'll always be there for you,
no matter where or why.

Katie Olbiks-Hill & Mollie Walters (10)
Sun Hill Junior School

Puddle Jumping

Puddles, what shape do they become?
They are all different sizes,
lots big, some small,
a few thin, fewer wide,
some the shape of a flower,
some the shape of a head,
most are the shape of the lakes,
flowing into the seas.

Abigail Pond (9)
Sun Hill Junior School

Super Chicken!

Super Chicken is the best,
He is better than the rest.
He fights and fights until he stops,
999, 'Oh no!' here come the cops.
Super Chicken is so fast,
He can go back into the past.
He can get so very mad,
When he has been very, very bad.
Super Chicken has magic powers,
He kicks bad guys up to high towers.
He pushes and punches really hard,
Until he received his birthday card.
Super Chicken, *it's his birthday!*
Hip, hip, hip, hooray.
I'm now 2,000 years old,
Now I have got five brand new powers.

Joe Dennehy (11) & Frainey Spurge (10)
Sun Hill Junior School

The Mystery of Super Fish

I wonder where my fish has gone,
I was so nice to him.
Maybe someone stole him
But I wonder who?
Maybe Super Cat
Or maybe Doctor Evil,
He might have just died,
But he's not in his tank.
I think I had fish last night,
Maybe that was Super Fish,
I think I ate Super Fish,
Oh no!

Oliver Bevan (10)
Sun Hill Junior School

Mystery Cat Is On The Case

I see the devil dog,
In the mist and fog,
I look around
And hear a sound,
Of the criminal cat!

I see some mud
And hear a giant thud,
It's from the stair,
Hope it's not a nightmare,
I need to go and explore.

I'm going to defeat
The criminal cat,
Even if it means throwing him out,
Onto the old mat,
I will!

Energy I need,
To help me succeed,
To defeat the criminal cat,
I am the Mystery Cat!

Chelsea Green & Kirsty Hamlen (10)
Sun Hill Junior School

Puddle Jumping

Nobody knows how a puddle is formed
Is it a dent in the ground?
Does a puddle make a splash?
A brilliant display of water
But when the sun comes it goes, where does it go?
I don't know
Will it come back?
I don't know.

Matthew Patrick (9)
Sun Hill Junior School

Super Chain Lady

The night has struck,
We hear a sound
Super Chain Lady circles the ground,
She lands on a roof and walks around,
Chh-chh-chh.
She jumps out at people,
They faint to the ground.
She chains them up, then swings them around,
Up they go then they fall back down,
Chh-chh-chh.
She walks back out onto the street,
Her chains following her as she greets,
Her next victim, there across the street.
Oh dear, oh dear, what can we do?
Will they escape the pains of the chains?
Chh-chh-chh!

Becky Page & Alice Burrows (10)
Sun Hill Junior School

Heroes

Superman is flying through the sky,
Spider-Man is climbing so high.
Batman, Robin, fighting Ivy,
But be quick her plants are lively.
A storm is brewing better watch out,
An X-man might be lurking about.
Four arms suddenly appear,
Fighting Doctor, OK it's Spider-Man, he's here!
Superman has met his match,
Spider-Man can swing and catch.
Now the time has come so near
It's time for us to disappear.

Naomi Barnett & Hayley Bennett (10)
Sun Hill Junior School

Superhero

I can move the thunderstorms
Direct it straight to someone's lawn
I can control electricity
Don't really get much publicity.
Give me the benefit of the doubt
I can save the whole world from drought
Now to my apprentice Tony Howl
All he does is sit there and cower.
Coming to defeat all the criminals
I hear people shout, 'Electrobe rules.'
My life hung on a dinner plate
What do I do? I go and eat it,
I've done everything now
Bored,
Bored,
Bored.

Ethan Wesley (10)
Sun Hill Junior School

Spider-Man's War

Spider-Man was having a rest,
Then in the window he saw a guest.
Spider-Man jumped up in fear,
He turned around and it was all clear.
He heard a creak coming from the door,
He looked and there was a mark on the floor.
He turned around and saw the Green Goblin in front of his eyes,
Suddenly it gave him a really big surprise.
They started fighting with all their might,
But to the Green Goblin it came as a fright.
Spider-Man had won the war
And kicked Green Goblin out of the door.

Katie Fisher & Charlie Holmes (11)
Sun Hill Junior School

Superhero

I love flying through the sky,
Just after you beat the bad guy.
A sudden burst of loop-the-loop,
I even went through an air-made hoop.
I thought it was all on my side,
Until I stopped my lovely glide.
Because I had a bad phone call,
I was not able to fly at all.
I had to go to a power station,
That made the propellers for my operation.
I need these things to fly in the sky,
I need these things to beat the bad guy.
But the station was broken beyond repair
And I wandered home with a costume that looked bare.

Daniel Lowman (10)
Sun Hill Junior School

Super Badger

Super Badger is so fast
He simply always powers past.
Super Badger is so strong
He's got muscles the size of Hong Kong.
Super Badger, he can fly
Way up high in the sky.
Super Badger is so cool
He's simply never scared when he meets rivals
Super Badger, his name is Aaron
His dad was the famous Ronny Sharon
Super Badger is so wise
That's why he simply never dies.

Alex Dale (11) & Aaron Fisher (10)
Sun Hill Junior School

Duck

I am out to catch Ard Varc Ratnie,
His intentions are to rule the world
And it's only me that stands between the world and total destruction.
Yes, it's Super Duck!
'What's that down there?
Dynamite under a railroad bridge
The evil work of Ard Varc Ratnie
This is a job for Super Duck.'
Grab it now before it's too late,
Zip up into the air,
I blow up but the bridge doesn't
You stupid Super Duck it's only a film set.
Flying over the sea and there is a ship sinking,
'Aha, the evil work of Ard Varc Ratnie,
This is a job for, you know who.'
I'll fly down and lift the bow above the surface again,
Suddenly I hear a boom and out comes a torpedo,
I am pushed along by the enormous force and then suddenly
Kaboom
Yes, it really is Super Duck!

Alex Penfold & Jamie Blanchard (10)
Sun Hill Junior School

The Tornado

Baby cries
It's getting closer
It's howling
It's screaming
Forests half destroyed
Baby cries even louder
Mother screams
House gone
Mother gone
Baby gone.

Charlotte Hurrell (9)
Sun Hill Junior School

Not A Breeze

I am a wind
In the early morning.
Not a breeze.
Not a hurricane.
I see an open bedroom window
Not a breeze.
Not a hurricane.
In I jump
And make *them* jump.
Not a breeze.
Not a breeze
But . . .
I decide to make havoc in the street
Not a breeze
But . . .
A Hurricane.

Susanna Diver (8)
Sun Hill Junior School

Sad

The whole world has fallen down on me
I have to hold it up
It's too heavy.

I am the only person on Earth
The only voice is mine
I am lonely.

I make a stream with my tears
I make a river flowing down
Every path and every road.

My heartbeat gets slower and slower
Like my soul has been taken away.

Anna Sulston (9)
Sun Hill Junior School

A Summer Breeze

The swaying flowers
Tickle my legs
During a summer breeze.
The delicate shimmer of wind
Tugs at the flowers
But stay very still.

The graceful trees are swinging,
In the delicate breeze.
The calm, warm wind
Whisks the leaves away.

The sweet-smelling flowers
Its scent in the air.
The soft wind brings dancing daisies
To fly around the sky
A stronger wind is coming I know.

The piles of golden brown leaves
Have been whipped
Out of the trees.
Now the sun is setting,
The last of the gentle summer breeze.

Olivia Probert (9)
Sun Hill Junior School

The Raging Wind

The leaves are falling
Heavily off their branches
Trees bending in two,
Bark crumbling to a heap
Leaves floating down, down, down
Blown all around
Dancing throughout the forest.

William Dennehy (9)
Sun Hill Junior School

Dancing Wind

Peaceful, whistling, twirling wind,
Breezy wind,
Pushing my hair.
Wind
Swaying trees
Flowing poppies.
The wind
Peaceful across my face
Cold and bitter.
Colourful sky, delicate and cold,
Dancing roses, twirling gently.
Breezy, wavy across the ocean
Peacefully whistling in the air
On a cold, summer's night.

Megan Lord (9)
Sun Hill Junior School

In The Forest

In the dark, gloomy forest,
The wind is howling,
The sky is pitch-black.
Except for the flash of lightning
Then the roaring wind starts to
Crash down.
Trees and bushes are
Being pulled up by the hurricane.
Sudden calm
There is nothing but a cold,
Quiet, bitter breeze
And
A destroyed forest.

Joshua Gates (8)
Sun Hill Junior School

Gentle Breeze

Gently blowing, getting strong
Feel it touch your face
Bitter cold, no . . . it's warm.
Is it snowing? Or is it a storm at sea?
No, neither.
It is gentle
It is swift
It is slow
It is a breeze.
Lightly blowing, swirling around you
Hitting your face
And smoothly touching your skin
It's going
It's gone
Now I'm warm
Maybe in the morning it will . . .
Return.

Jessica Arrowsmith (8)
Sun Hill Junior School

The Wind

Is a storm coming?
Is it the wind?
It's turning into a tornado
It's whipping up houses and cars.
It's coming
Heading for the
Mountain top
Where we are
Run, run!
It's coming for us.
Too late!
We are sucked up by the tornado.

Sophie Fairbairn (8)
Sun Hill Junior School

Lightning

L ightning bolt through the sky, hear the scream when people cry.
I n the night a flash of light, hide under your covers with fright.
G o run before this lightning bolt strikes.
H urry, run, get away otherwise you will be ashes.
T ime for lightning in the sky.
N ear you, ready or not.
I n your garden.
N ear your house.
G et ready, it's about to strike. Too late, you're dead.

Sharni Gibbs (9)
Sun Hill Junior School

The Wind

The wind moans
The wind groans
It grumbles
It crashes
It smashes
Against nature.
It twists and whirls
It turns the boys and girls
Into space and upside down.

Madeline Quirk (9)
Sun Hill Junior School

Tornado

A tornado sucks
A tornado spins
A tornado twirls in the wind
It plucks up homes
It destroys forests and cities.

Brett Sawyer & Tom Hanks (8)
Sun Hill Junior School

Winter Wind

A stormy night down at the beach,
A grey sky
With snow drifting down covering the trees.

Crash!
A tree gets hit by lightning,
The wind is getting angrier and angrier
Whipping up the sea.

Whining, whistling sound deafens you
Sand blows in your face,
A bright light zigzags in the sky.

Jack Messenger (8)
Sun Hill Junior School

Puddle Jumping

I see a puddle I want to jump
I jump! I splash!
The puddle is as big as a river
The water flows up and down
The sky goes dark
I jump, I'm over
The sky goes light
The river turns back home again!

Claire Matheson (9)
Sun Hill Junior School

Puddle Jumping

P uddles are fun
U p and down we jump
D ips in the playground
D own on playground they're fun
L ower playground madness
E normous puddles are all around.

Haydn Jones (9)
Sun Hill Junior School

Two Days

S chool is boring in the rain, please go away.
C ause it is the most wettest rain of my life
H ello, I meet my friends at the school gates.
O h no, the rain is back again!
O h yes, there's the sun in the sky, bright and high.
L earning is good in the sun.
D on't come back again
A s the sun is coming out
Y es, the sun's out I can have a good day again
S oggy and wet as the rain goes on all day long.

Harry Nugent (9)
Sun Hill Junior School

Blasting Wind

Round and round the velodrome
The cyclist trailing the wind.
Blasting, blasting, swooping
Round and round the velodrome.

Round and round the velodrome
The cyclist increases the speed.
Faster and faster, the wind is blasting
Beating into the face.

Harvey Watson (8)
Sun Hill Junior School

Puddle Jumping

Puddles are big, puddles are small
Sometimes deep, maybe dirty
Good to jump in, sometimes not fun at all
You get wet all day through
The little drops shining as they fall.

Kaylie Grace (9)
Sun Hill Junior School

My Puddle

My puddle is shaped all strange,
The size of it is huge.
Bigger than my swimming pool,
Bigger than a river,
Seaweed grows beneath my puddle,
Like branches on a tree,
This golden sand grows beneath me,
Like the sun glistening with me,
With people laughing and having fun,
Like some birds playing in the sun.

Ashleigh Wilmot (10)
Sun Hill Junior School

Puddle Jumping

On the playground
Puddles everywhere.
Mud, leaves and water
Mixed together
Water is healthy for you
You can take a bath.

Makayla Bannister (9)
Sun Hill Junior School

Tornado

It whirls,
It twirls,
It swirls,
It sucks up trees
Like a wresting match
It is as strong as a titanium steel wall.

Peter Amey (8)
Sun Hill Junior School

Yesterday

Yesterday was burnt, like an open fire,
Today is fresh, like pure-cold water.
Yesterday was boiling, like a desert plain,
Today is pouring, like buckets of water.
Yesterday was sweating, like a hot bath,
Today is frozen, like a snowdrop flame.
Yesterday was breathtaking, like another world,
Today is all grey, like some trays.
Yesterday was bright, like a school light bulb,
Today is damp, like a paddling pool.
Yesterday was a no wind day, like a broken fan,
Today is cloudy, like a smoke machine.

Celeste Richards (9)
Sun Hill Junior School

Yesterday And Today

Yesterday was bright and sunny
Today is dull and wet.
Yesterday was fun and happy
Today is not like that.
Yesterday we could go out and play
Today inside is where we have to stay.
Yesterday was hot and dry
Today is cold and wet.
Yesterday was nearly too hot
Today thunder rules the sky.
Yesterday was bright and sunny
Today is dull and wet.

Nicola Fry (9)
Sun Hill Junior School

The Wind Makes Me Feel . . .

The wind makes me feel relaxed,
Like an angel in the breeze.

The wind makes me feel dramatic,
Like a tree swaying in the gentle atmosphere.

The wind makes me feel silent,
Like a cat with its glowing eyes.

The wind makes me feel calm,
Like a statue not making a move.

The wind makes me feel delicate,
Like a marionette on strings.

The wind makes me feel airy,
Like a fan blowing gently.

Alexander Dobner (8)
Sun Hill Junior School

The Superhero

The Superhero swings from tree to tree,
Wondering what evil there ever shall be.

The Superhero swims like a fish in the lake,
Wondering *why* people's lives are at stake.

The Superhero climbs thinking, *this is a fake*
Wondering if innocent are grateful he spake.

The Superhero destroys the evil world
Wondering if *all* evil has yet uncurled.

The Superhero rescues the innocent folk,
Knowing that evil has at last been broke.

Naomi-Jane Andrews (10)
Sun Hill Junior School

Puddle Jumping

Jump, jump, jump, splash!

As you jump over the puddles as quick as a click,
When the ants sit there with a puzzled face,
Thinking how do they do it
A puddle to an ant is an *ocean*
Full of slimy seaweed and
Fish that eat each other . . .
But a puddle to us is just
A dip in the ground
With bits of dead grass and
Creatures that we can't even see!

Emily Milburn (9)
Sun Hill Junior School

Puddle Jumping

P uddles can be big and small,
U ntil they dry up,
D own a waterfall they don't dry up.
D anger too far in the sea,
L ook out there in the sea, it's a shark.
E els live in the sea
S eas are the biggest puddles in the world.

Lewis Markwick (10)
Sun Hill Junior School

The Wind

The wind moans and then it groans
It grumbles, it crashes,
It smashes against nature.
It twists and twirls,
It turns the boys and girls
Upside down.

Milo Ogus, Ashley Burnett & Matthew James (8)
Sun Hill Junior School

Puddle Jumping

Today's not a hot day
Today's not a cold day
Today's a damp day.

I went to the playground and picked a puddle
My puddle is shaped like the number eight.

When I zoom out I can see my puddle
In the centre of loads of other puddles
All different shapes, all different sizes.

If I move even more away
I can see everyone puddle jumping.

Hettie Whale (9)
Sun Hill Junior School

Puddle Jumping

P uddles are fun to jump in, but sometimes they're not
U p, up and away
D azzling, shiny drops of rain becoming huge puddles to jump in.
D ropping down from the clouds.
L ittle puddles on the ground, a car comes along, runs it over, flat puddle
E ven bigger as it gets more cars run over it and more people jump in it.

William Turner (10)
Sun Hill Junior School

Puddle Jumping

The world is a puddle
The sea is the biggest puddle in the world.

Puddle jumping is so cool
You get to get as wet as you want
And it's just like the sea.

Liam Forcey (10)
Sun Hill Junior School

My Superhero Powers

Whenever I fly,
Like a bird in the sky,
I'm always afraid in the end,
Sometimes I really can't defend.
My laser eyes are running out,
You're bored without a doubt
My super powers are really fading
Do you want to go rollerblading?
Smarty girl dumped me,
By the old oak tree,
From your son
Who's going to flee.

Esther Southwick (10)
Sun Hill Junior School

Roboboy

R eading only memory,
O nly made to fight crime,
B eing alert for villains striking,
O n and off all day and night.
B ouncing into action in a split second,
O ffering his help whenever it's needed,
Y oung robot superhero, saving the world.

Alexander Arrowsmith (10)
Sun Hill Junior School

The Mistral

It was as rough as the stormy sea
As powerful as a tiger
It speeds like a rocket into the air
It sucked up the trees and threw them into the air.

Abbie Hughes & Nadia Hansford (8)
Sun Hill Junior School

Lightning

L ikely to make your nose bleed with a punch.
I incredibly strong and a lot of muscle.
G eared up and ready to fight.
H andy when it comes to powers.
T ight clothes all the days of the week.
N ight watchman.
I ntelligent and clean.
N aughty when he is destroying things with his lightning beams.
G ood when he helps people in trouble.

Nicholas Coles (10)
Sun Hill Junior School

Puddle Jumping

Water means everything to us.
If water did not fall, we would not exist.
If water did not fall, plants would not exist.
If water did not fall, the streams would not exist.
If water did not fall, lakes would not exist.
If water did not fall, oceans would not exist.
If water did not fall, the world would not exist.

Calum Sheppard (9)
Sun Hill Junior School

Puddle Jumping

P uddles can be fun, who knows when they'll come,
U mbrellas up everyone, time to have some fun.
D oes it come every day?
D o it while you can.
L ife is rain when it comes,
E veryone it's raining, time to have some fun.

Nathan Humphrey (9)
Sun Hill Junior School

Super Monkey!

S winging down the corridor,
U p the stairs and onto the floor.
P ut my cape on, 1, 2, 3.
E veryone thinks the world of me,
R ight! Ready for action!

M ighty me, swing through the trees,
O ver the bridge, 1, 2, 3.
N ot me who did this, not me who did that.
K nock over the man who stole my hat.
E verest isn't tough for me
Y es, that's me *Super Monkey!*

Laura Hogg, Abigail Dailly & Chelsea Lane (10)
Sun Hill Junior School

The Blob

T he Blob was a superhero,
H e wobbled like jelly,
E xtremely fat is The Blob.

B lob flies like a bomb,
L ikes to save people
O nly he can't,
B lob is not as good as others.

Matthew Waite & Stefan Clarkson (10)
Sun Hill Junior School

Breezy Wind

It was a breezy wind at the beach in daytime.
It was a calm and floating wind there,
Then it started to whistle.
Got cold and the sea stopped.

Danielle Messer (8)
Sun Hill Junior School

Spider-Man

S pider-Man swings from trees and buildings.
P eople watch him swing and swing,
   fighting crime at the midnight scene
I deas appear in my head like seeing the Green Goblin dead.
D aring people arrive in my head like hoping the Green Goblin dead.
E lectrical wires exploding in the night,
   wondering if I should go and fight?
R ight, time for bed, wonder what will happen in my dream tonight?

M en see me fight and fight, wondering what I'll do tonight
A little boy said, 'What were you doing last night?'
   I swung away and said, 'Night-night.'
N ight-night to you as well.

Jordan Pitter (10)
Sun Hill Junior School

Caramel Girl

C aramel Girl saves people with her sticky caramel hand.
A girl who loves caramel and people just love her. It's
R eally scary when Caramel is around, so beware
A nd when you get saved, she gives you a caramel bar.
M elting Caramel Girl will melt if she gets hot,
E nergy Caramel Girl needs,
L ove and care is what Caramel loves.

G irly girl, that's a superhero
I just love the way her hand turns to caramel
R ed, white, green and blue, I love gold for Caramel
L ovely Caramel, so when you see Caramel Girl,
   just shout, 'Caramel!'

Sophie Carey (10)
Sun Hill Junior School

The Powerful Wind

The wind is rough and powerful,
It struggles through the trees.
It's so powerful,
It could knock your house down.
It rushes through created nature.
The wind is mean,
The wind is strong,
It's angry,
It speeds up,
So powerful.
It turns into a tornado
It moans
It cries through the howling air.

Lucy Watson (8)
Sun Hill Junior School

Tornado

It swirls
It twirls
It whirls
It sucks up houses and trees
Like it is in a wrestling match

It is strong
It is mean
It is rough
It is moaning
It twists
The pressure is rising
Beware of the tornado.

Megan Aynsley (8)
Sun Hill Junior School

Arctic Winds

In the cold Arctic the polar bear and her cubs go in their den,
The wind is coming
The wind is coming
The Arctic fox curls up snug
The wind is coming
The wind is coming
The emperor penguins huddle up tight
The wind is coming
The wind is coming
The bitter polar winds have come
I feel a shiver down my spine,
So do they
The polar winds have come!

Thomas Brookes (8)
Sun Hill Junior School

Strong Wind

It starts off as a breeze
And now it knocks sugar canes.
It gets stronger and stronger
Until it turns into a hurricane.

The hurricane blows up cars
And hurricane Francis visits Florida.
Stronger and stronger and stronger
It is now as strong as a titanium steel wall.

Zachariah Gilmore & James Page (8)
Sun Hill Junior School

The Wind

The wind follows you around
Not just one place.
It doesn't leave you alone,
Sometimes it is annoying.

Frances Jarvis (8)
Sun Hill Junior School

Yesterday and Today

Yesterday was way too hot,
The sunbeams danced around.
The birds were singing,
The world was ringing,
With lots of beautiful sounds.

Now today is way too wet.
The raindrops drumming on the ground.
The streams are growing,
They might be overflowing,
It seems all clean and fresh.

One day we are complaining,
Because we're getting sunburn,
The next day we're too cold.
Let's make up our minds,
Find one nobody minds,
Why can't the weather be just right?

Clodagh McSweeney (9)
Sun Hill Junior School

The Irish Dude

I 'm an Irish man
R eady to fight crime
I n the United Kingdom
S itting on a hot dog
H itting criminals with my trusty Irish stick

D onkey kung fu me down
U p comes the Irish dude
D own to the donkey dudes
E merald eye vision shooting in every direction!

George Long & Bobby Matthews (10)
Sun Hill Junior School

The Howling Wind

The wind howls like a pack of wolves
On the Grand Canyon.
You know it is the dreaded wind
Because the leaves rustle.
You can see the tornado in the distance
Birds are fleeing from their nests.
it crashes buildings down, sweeping up
Houses, while the people run for cover.

Thomas Waite & James Timberlake (8)
Sun Hill Junior School

Spin Wind

Leaves trembling
Apples falling
Trees tumbling down
Houses vanishing
Cars blowing away
Tornados spinning and rattling
Plants pulled up from the ground
And things flying around.

Rebecca Simpson & Emily Biehn (8)
Sun Hill Junior School

Wind

How strong is the wind?
Nobody knows.
The breeze is as light as a feather.
The wind then whistles,
The gale forces across the sea.
Lastly the tornado
Explodes fully.

James Harrison & Samuel Wilson (8)
Sun Hill Junior School

The Spinning Tornado!

The spinning tornado's forcing everything off the ground.
Picking up tall trees and huge houses.
Spinning like a vortex in the swimming pool.
Howling at the window, rattling the panes
And slamming every door shut.
Swirling, twirling, dancing through keyholes
Making mischief for everyone.

Jenni Stokes, Emma Welford & Cassie Joss (8)
Sun Hill Junior School

Beach Wind

The warm, bouncy wind flew over the top
Of the great, big, busy, wild waves.

The wind is blown out to sea,
Further, further and further,
Until it reached a deserted island
The wind gets stronger, stronger still.

Mighty, powerful, raging wind.

Pascale Chalmers-Arnold (8)
Sun Hill Junior School

Storm Wind

It's a wild storm
The sky is lit up in the cold air.
The storm blistering through the trees,
Inside the gloomy forest.
Crash!
The trees are tumbling down, down.
The cars are driving by.

James Masters (8)
Sun Hill Junior School

Yesterday Today

Yesterday I could see the sun as bright as shining, shimmering gold.
I could feel the sun beating down on me like fiery heat balls.
I could taste the wind lightly playing across my tongue,
like a fan turned down low.
I could hear birds twittering merrily to each other
like nothing could go wrong.
I could smell the scent of happiness throughout the school.
However, today I can see windows splattered in rain
like someone does not want us to see out.
I can feel the bitter glumness of misery
throughout the school like it will never end.
I can taste the rain dropping onto my tongue like it would never stop.
I can hear the cry of the plants as they fight against strong winds.
I can smell the fresh smell of waterlogged grass
like they took a cold shower.
So I hope tomorrow it will not be either of these, but in-between.

Matthew Moss (9)
Sun Hill Junior School

Wind Poem

The leaves are rustling
They're jumping, jumping like a gazelle.
The wind is getting stronger and stronger
The branches are swaying
From side to side.
Harder and harder the wind blows,
Branches are falling.
I'm getting colder and colder.
I'm cycling faster and faster.
Eventually I get home.
Everyone is hiding under the bed.

Karl Stevens (8)
Sun Hill Junior School

Yesterday, Today

Y esterday was hot and sunny
E veryone loved it
S ometimes we got a bit hot
T he sun was very bothering
E veryone was tired of work and
R eady to go out to play
D readful the heat was, it tired us out
A worse day is coming so
Y ou should get your coats ready.

T oday it's very rainy
O h why did it have to rain?
D readful weather
A lthough it's nice after yesterday's climate
Y es, it will get worse.

Alec Thorne (9)
Sun Hill Junior School

Whirling Wind

The wind is twisting and twirling around me
Like a spinning whirlpool.
I try to catch it in my net
But I miss, for it is too frisky.
Cool breeze, winding round my face.
I think I'm in a different place.
Flying around, but not to be found, going round.
The curly, whirly, swirly wind wraps
Around plants and trees.
It brushes my hair back like a broom
Floating in mid-air
So wild and wispy
Too frisky to last.

Jessica Powell (8)
Sun Hill Junior School

The Howling Wind

The wind is soft
Now it's angry
Angrier and angrier,
Now the wind is howling.
Howling like mad.
Ripping trees out of the ground
Houses crumbling
Knocking down buildings
The wind is noisier, louder
It's hitting my back, I feel cold.

Charlotte Wills (8)
Sun Hill Junior School

The Tornado

The swooping wind hit the trees,
The trees bending in the air roaring,
Leaves are flying everywhere.
Doors are slamming,
The animals' homes tumble down,
Rain hails into the ground.
Then it stops
Everything is ruined!

Aidan Pond (8)
Sun Hill Junior School

Lightning

Lighting, lightning shocking
Quick, your head could be off with one spark
Beware, beware of the little click
You could be in all shapes and sizes
Beware, beware of the dreaded form
It could kill you.

Toby Hartshorn (9)
Sun Hill Junior School

Hurricane

Round and round
Houses, trees, people, pets
Frightened and ruined
Gardens ripped to pieces,
Here it comes
Round and round
Picking everything up
Crash!
Bang!

Jessica Blanchard (8)
Sun Hill Junior School

Wild Wind

The wild wind came raging in,
Pushing, shoving to and fro,
It flung the books off bookcases
And heaved the silver night!

Everything was ruined
Everything was destroyed
It was a disaster

Oh, will it happen again?

Ellie Grant (8)
Sun Hill Junior School

Golden Leaves

When you're in the woods at dawn
The breeze hits your face,
With arches of golden leaves
Snowing like Christmas
Children come out to play,
They roll through the great piles of golden leaves,
Then the breeze follows you through the door.

Peter Barnett (9)
Sun Hill Junior School

Lightning

The strike of death
From the skies of Hell
The innocent crying for mercy
And then . . . pain and death.

The skies are silent
Every move is intense
The sun is here
Heaven is upon us.

Rosalind Jones (9)
Sun Hill Junior School

Angels

Angels, angels everywhere
Angels, angels over there
Late at night when I'm in bed
I see them in my daddy's shed
I'm running down St Stephen's street
Hoping that I can meet an angel

Angel, angel in the air
Angel, angel with long, blonde hair
Angel, angel, you're so bright
To guide me through the long, cold night

Angels, angels everywhere
Angels, angels over there
I wake at night and stop and stare
Oh my god, there's an angel there
I said, 'Hello,' and shook her hand
And wished her well, back to Never Land.

Becky Hart (10)
Townhill Junior School

Why Aren't They Just Like Me?

I'm just a normal little girl,
So happy, fun-loving and carefree.
They hurt so many people,
Why aren't they just like me?

The Russian children went to school,
Their first day back, so happy!
Many lives were shattered and ruined,
Why aren't they just like me?

Out to play on their own,
Were Jessica and Holly,
Never again because of nasty people,
Why aren't they just like me?

Bombs on trains, planes and cars,
There are far too many.
These people are so bad and nasty,
Why aren't they just like me?

The Americans got onto planes,
Flew through the air so free.
They took over the planes and crashed into the buildings,
Why aren't they just like me?

I go to gym and make cakes with my grandma,
And go about with my friends happily.
I care about what happens in our world,
I wish they were just like me!

Summer Fancett (9)
Townhill Junior School

Rain

Rain, rain's all around up and down through the town.
It rains on my umbrella
It rains on a tree
It even rains on the ships at sea
But does not rain on me.

Danielle Nixon (9)
Townhill Junior School

Chocolate Cake

Chocolate cake is my favourite food
I love chocolate, so should you!

It's sweet and tasty, good and fun,
Tangy and smooth and liked by everyone.
It's made from cocoa and from milk
And the sugar syrup tastes like silk.

Some with raisins, some with cream,
You can have whatever you dream.
A cherry on top and jam in the middle,
The thought of it makes me dribble.

I can't help it, I'm a chocoholic,
I could eat it when I sleep, even when I vomit.

Chocolate . . . *mmmmmmmmm!*

Clarese Winwood (7)
Townhill Junior School

Fat And Thin

The sumo wrestler tummy is
Like a blow-up ball
But the gymnast is tiny
Like a flag post is really tall.

The burgers are selling
Like tickets to see Busted
But the baby bananas are curving
And they're really nice with custard.

The loaf of bread is big
Like a juicy plum
But the ruler is thin
Like a baby's tiny thumb.

Rebecca Quilter (11)
Townhill Junior School

The Great Misfortunes of Humpty Dumpty

Humpty Dumpty was a great egg,
He dropped a spanner on top of his head,
The shell cracked and the white started to spout
And then, at last, the yolk came out.

Humpty Dumpty swallowed a bee,
He screamed, he cried, he shouted, 'Mummy!'
He's always had a sting in his throat,
When he goes to the dentist he looks quite remote.

Humpty Dumpty went sailing one day,
An octopus came and took him away,
He tried to fight and stay afloat,
When his friend Marcus pulled him back to the boat.

Humpty Dumpty sat on a cactus,
He cried and kicked a duck-billed platypus,
But the hole in his trousers he couldn't sew back,
So his bottom was shown in the cotton wool lack.

Humpty Dumpty was kicked by a horse,
He screamed, shouted and cursed of course,
He went to the hospital sucking his thumb,
He lived, but he lived with a wound on his bum.

Humpty Dumpty went to Jamaica,
He wanted to eat some mashed potato,
There was none of it, not even a bit,
He was so upset he jumped in a pit.
At the bottom he found a squealing pig,
He cooked it over a burning twig,
He ate a lot, but saved some for later,
When he hoped to have found his mashed potato.

Joseph Venable (9)
Townhill Junior School

Once Upon A Rhyme

Once upon a rhyme there was a teacher called Miss Gregory.
She was the prettiest teacher in TJS,
Then Mr Crossley shouting at crimes,
He's always making a mess and trying to play chess.
After that there is Miss Stone, she is the most reliable teacher,
She teaches us methods that even our parents wouldn't understand.
Then Miss Barley, she is amazingly clever,
I bet she can do a handstand!
Now for Miss Garrod, she's the best at science,
She loves sorting out word problems a lot.
Miss Child does fun activities with us, she is also fantastic at art.
Miss Fox is so foxy with her lovely red hair,
She tells us lovely stories about 'Maximous' and his friends.
Mr Batchelor is always telling us the rules so we are safe.
But what he did not tell us, is if we are allowed to wear contact lenses.

Juanita Jordan (8)
Townhill Junior School

Once Upon A Rhyme

Gymnastics is fun, it is good for everyone.
Trampolining, the bars, beams and vaults,
All technical stuff that I love.
Practice, practice, practice is the only way to be perfect.
Aches in my back, aches in my legs,
Aches, aches everywhere,
All part of the fun of being a good gymnast.
Training two or three times a week and on weekends too.
Missing lots of parties, just to get through.
But I know one day, all the hard work will pay.
I'll be at the Olympics saying, 'Hip hip hooray!'

Julia Jordan (8)
Townhill Junior School

Conkers

Conkers are as hard as jewels,
But not as bouncy as bouncy balls.
They can fit in your pocket,
But not in your locket.
They're smooth and round,
There's one on the ground.
They're as brown as a bear,
Conkers, conkers,
They're *everywhere!*

Jade McLean (10)
Townhill Junior School

Colours Of The Rainbow

Red is the colour of our school jumpers.
Orange is the colour of the flames in the fire.
Yellow is the colour of sunflowers in the garden.
Green is the colour of grasshoppers hidden in the grass.
Blue is the colour of the sky above where the rainbow lies.
Indigo is the colour of my school folder that I keep my work in.
Violet is the colour that makes me happy.

Demi Naismith (8)
Townhill Junior School

Horses

Horses gallop round and round
Horses gallop over the ground.
They canter through the forest gate
Hoping they will not be late.
To jump across the fallen logs
And to run away from vicious dogs.

Emily Dowling (10)
Townhill Junior School

Evil Grannies

Evil grannies make you starve to death or fill you to the brim.
Then when they're finished with you they make an evil grin.

Evil grannies make you work hard, until you're turning blue
And even when you're bursting, you can't go to the loo.

Evil grannies are just plain mean and need to give you a break,
But when your work is over they poison your chocolate cake.

Evil grannies are annoying, they really are a pain.
They wind me up so much that I'd like to act the same.

Evil grannies really scare me when they smile in their granny way,
But I really wish that evil grin would disappear and they would go away.

I wish the old dragon would just go and pack,
But what I really want most is my parents back!

Sarah Chun (10)
Townhill Junior School

Sadness

A rose's tears
fall as petals,
as they glide to the ground,
never to be heard.

A puppy's whimper,
Full of sadness and pain,
Travels for miles on end,
Only to be heard
And regretted.

So take each chance you get,
Be faithful to your friends,
Take your life to the limit,
Because sadness is all around us
And there's nothing we can do to stop it.

Georgina Diffey (10)
Townhill Junior School

My Pets

Mothball, my horse,
Ran the racecourse,
I was so proud,
And I shouted so loud,
That I was left feeling hoarse!

Gypsy, my cat,
Sat on her mat,
She left us a mouse,
In the middle of our house,
Lucky it wasn't a rat!

Ginger, my guinea pig,
Is fluffy but big,
He runs round his cage,
In a mad rage,
Looks like he's doing a jig.

Kirsty Hunt (9)
Townhill Junior School

Dolphins

Dolphins, dolphins, how wonderful they are.

Swimming up, swimming down,
Swimming gracefully round and round.

Just like me they like to play
I'd like to swim with them one day.

Leaping in the air
Diving down into the sea.

I live on land
They live in the sea.

That's the difference between them and me.

Milly Ann Mintram (7)
Townhill Junior School

Dolphins

Dolphins always have smiles on their faces,
Their skin is so silky they always sing to you.
They are lovely, they will let you swim with them
And when you go they will blow you a kiss goodbye.
Dolphins are friendly, when they jump they will see the stars,
When you have upset them they swim away
And you will never see them again.
I love dolphins I hope you do
Dolphins' eyes are like diamonds
And one day I want to swim with the biggest *dolphin*.

Brodie Wheeler-Osman (9)
Townhill Junior School

My Birthday

My birthday sign is Pisces.
My birthday was exciting.
We had an all night party.
We chatted in the moonlight
And stayed up all night.
We went for a swim in a cold pool.
We had a hot dog, chips and a big slice of cake!
I opened my presents and got what I wanted,
A big fluffy rabbit with big, floppy ears.

Jasmin Urquhart (8)
Townhill Junior School

101 Dalmatians

101 Dalmatians, what a big sensation!
Instead of dogs, why not frogs?
'Cause they can leap across the street
And get me something to eat.
How neat!

Katie Cluett (10)
Townhill Junior School

On The School Roof . . .

On the roof there was . . . A . . . A . . . A . . . angry angels
On the roof there was . . . B . . . B . . . B . . . bouncing balls
On the roof there was . . . C . . . C . . . C . . . creepy-crawlies
On the roof there was . . . D . . . D . . . D . . . diving doves

On the roof there was not . . . E . . . E . . . E . . . eleven eggs
On the roof there was not . . . F . . . F . . . F . . . flying friends
On the roof there was not . . . G . . . G . . . G . . . grumpy grandads
On the roof there was not . . . H . . . H . . . H . . . horrific horses

On the roof there should not be . . . I . . . I . . . I . . . icy igloos
On the roof there should not be . . . J . . . J . . . J . . . jumping jumpers
On the roof there should not be . . . K . . . K . . . K . . . kickboxing kangaroos
On the roof there should not be . . . L . . . L . . . L . . . large leopards

On the roof there should be . . . M . . . M . . . M . . . mucky mud
On the roof there should be . . . N . . . N . . . N . . . noisy nightingales
On the roof there should be . . . O . . . O . . . O . . . oblong objects
On the roof there should be . . . P . . . P . . . P . . . plastic planes

On the roof there is . . . Q . . . Q . . . Q . . . quacking quails
On the roof there is . . . R . . . R . . . R . . . raging rainstorms
On the roof there is . . . S . . . S . . . S . . . slippery slates
On the roof there is . . . T . . . T . . . T . . . tremendous tarantulas

On the roof there is not . . . U . . . U . . . U . . . unhappy unicorns
On the roof there is not . . . V . . . V . . . V . . . vicious vampires
On the roof there is not . . . W . . . W . . . W . . . waltzing walrus
On the roof there is not . . . X . . . X . . . X . . . xiphoid xylophones

On the roof there might be . . . Y . . . Y . . . Y . . . yellow yachts
On the roof there might be . . . Z . . . Z . . . Z . . . zigzag zebras.

Ryan Hunt (8)
Townhill Junior School

The Spider And The Fly

Through the colours of the garden,
Death hidden away,
Down the sweet, calm stream,
Towards the unknown dismay,
Up the church spire,
Down the hole inside,
There beneath the psalter,
The spider shot out the lace
And the fly was up the winding stair.

Into the spider's parlour, but not out.
It came back to hunt the beast.

His heart was in the web,
When it came back, he was very much *dead!*

David Harrold (9)
Westbourne Primary School

The Spider And The Fly

Sneaky spider, dumb fly
Web soaring through the sky
Eyes as dark as a moonless night
Spider so creepy causes a fright.

Fly through the misty night
I land on the doorstep
Of the spider in the night fright.
He grabs me and takes me up his winding stair,
I scream to give him a shock
He drops me on the webbed floor
And I quickly flutter out the door.
Never again will I go into his parlour.

Charlotte Leach (9)
Westbourne Primary School

The Earth From The Harvest Moon

I see a planet of green, blue and white
shining brightly in the night
from the seas to the land
from the land to air
life is everywhere!
At the bottom of the deep
even there life does not sleep.
Where there is the greatest heat
life remains on its feet
even in the bitter cold
life still has a firm hold
then there are the skies above
they are reached by a dove.

Life is ever changing
but for now it's beautiful
for the planet is Earth
as viewed from the harvest moon.

Matthew Cowen (9)
Westbourne Primary School

Leaves

Falling leaves like raindrops.
Leaves are brownish gold in autumn.
Leaves lose hold of their branches.
Leaves feel like crunchy, scrunched-up newspaper.
Leaves look like ginger hair.
Autumn leaves everywhere.

Ashley Airton (7)
Westbourne Primary School

The World's Wonders

Look around you, what do you see?
A high, soaring eagle,
A low, buzzing bee,
From the tiny, small ant
To the great, big, blue whale.
Stop, look around you, what do you see?
A dirty, city pigeon
Or a white turtle dove,
A small bony mouse
To a great, grizzly bear.
A fast-swimming dolphin,
Or a sly, greedy fox.
Stop, look around you, what do you see?
How long will these wonders stay on our Earth?
So care for the cats, the dogs and the fleas.
Just please look after these things.

Zak Conlon (9)
Westbourne Primary School